THE WEED RUNNERS

Travels with the Outlaw Capitalists of America's Medical Marijuana Trade

NICHOLAS SCHOU

CHICAGO
REVIEW
PRESS

Portions of this book previously appeared in *OC Weekly*
First edition
Published by Chicago Review Press, Incorporated
814 North Franklin Street
Chicago, Illinois 60610

ISBN 978-1-61374-410-9

Cover design: Matt Simmons
Interior design: Sarah Olson

Library of Congress Cataloging-in-Publication Data
Schou, Nick.
   The weed runners : travels with the outlaw capitalists and modern-day
bootleggers of America's medical marijuana trade / Nicholas Schou.—First edition.
      pages cm
   Includes index.
   Summary: "Drawing on unparalleled access to sources ranging from doctors
and lawyers to lobbyists, cannabis club owners, outlaw cultivators, and industry
entrepreneurs, The Weed Runners is both journalistic expose and adventure story.
The book's title refers to those who run the vast network fueling the ongoing
nationwide explosion of medical marijuana. Focusing on an incredibly dynamic
three-year period from 2009 to 2012, this fast-moving and exciting portrait
examines the lives of the people involved in today's marijuana trade and recent
developments in the federal war on medical marijuana. Unlike other books on
the topic, this narrative gives readers a first-hand account on America's quasi-legal
medical marijuana trade"—Provided by publisher.
   Summary: "A behind-the-scenes look at the quasi-legal business of medical
marijuana and the people who risk their liberty to push the limits of this grand
experiment"—Provided by publisher.
   ISBN 978-1-61374-410-9 (pbk.)
   1. Marijuana--Therapeutic use—United States. 2. Drug legalization—United
States. 3. Lobbying—United States. 4. Marijuana industry—United States. I. Title.

   RM666.C266S36 2013
   362.29'5—dc23

                              2013011343

Printed in the United States of America
5 4 3 2 1

THE WEED RUNNERS

Contents

Acknowledgments

Writing a book about the inner workings of America's marijuana industry, where the lines between what is legal and what is not so legal are so blurry as to defy definition, is no easy task. By definition, however, the risks facing the subjects of such a manuscript are far greater than those faced by the writer. Therefore, I'd like to thank everyone who spoke to me for this book and who helped me with my coverage of the medical marijuana movement for *OC Weekly* over the past sixteen years.

Many of these sources appear in this book, although for obvious reasons and where clearly stated, I couldn't always use their real names. I'd also like to thank my editor and partner in crime at the *Weekly*, Gustavo Arellano, for his support of my efforts, as well as Voice Media Group for giving me permission to use previously published material from my years of work on this project. As always, thanks also to my literary agent, Jill Marsal, and to my wife, Claudia, for her guidance and support.

Introduction

It might be a stretch to say that the history of America's underground marijuana trade is encapsulated in the story of Donald Hoxter.

Not by much, though.

Few people can say they've smuggled as much as ten tons of marijuana across both the Mexican and Canadian borders per year. Or that they were one of the first hippies in the Pacific Northwest to pioneer America's homegrown crop in the early 1980s, some fifteen years before marijuana became legal, first in California, and then in more than a dozen other states, for medical purposes. And it's certainly true that few have won or lost as much as Hoxter in this business. His story, which ends before the tales contained in this book begin, is therefore a perfect place to start.

At the moment, Hoxter is sitting at an outdoor table at a coffee shop in Long Beach, California, at a busy intersection, kitty-corner from an elementary school where kids are loudly enjoying their afternoon recess. He's a tall, lanky man in his early sixties with whitening red hair and freckles. His fair skin is mottled red and white, permanently scorched by forty-one straight months in the too-sunny recreation yard of a federal prison. A fresh cigarette dangles from his lips. He's almost lit the thing several times over the past hour or so, but instead absentmindedly twirls the lighter with his left hand.

Hoxter is too busy talking to smoke. The memories, some of which are still a jumble in his mind since he hasn't spoken publicly about much of his life until now, overflow. It all started in the early 1960s, he says, when he was a kid in El Cajon, a gritty, working-class town just east of San Diego. Then as now, El Cajon was a bastion of the Hells Angels, and several members of the outlaw motorcycle gang happened to live on the street where Hoxter grew up. "They lived on the same block, much to my mother's chagrin," remembers Hoxter. "I got my first joint from the Hells Angels. They cost about four for a dollar back then. And of course they came from Mexico. Mexico is where everything came from in the beginning."

Hoxter hung out with older kids and young adults who tended to drive down to Tijuana each weekend. He didn't realize it right away, but a lot of them weren't just crossing the border to get drunk in the cantinas of the infamous Zona Norte. "A friend of mine came back one time, and was laughing and joking and opened up the trunk of his Chevrolet," he recalls. The friend lifted up some unfolded newspapers and proudly showed Hoxter several bricks of cheap Mexican grass. Even before Hoxter was old enough to drive, he was going along for the ride, and by the time he had his license, he was a smuggler. "It was nothing. You just drove down and drove back," he recalls. "Going into Mexico, there was no police presence, and coming back you just played it like you had gotten drunk because that's what people did."

Typically, Hoxter and his friends would find a back-alley dealer, pool their money, and purchase about two pounds of pot that had been packed into tight bundles, or bricks. Each one cost $60 or $70.

Then they'd sell each pound for $300, dividing the amount into thirty lids, or $10 quantities, which were measured by a finger's width of a Prince Albert can of tobacco. By the late 1960s, he and his buddies were handling much larger loads, thirty or forty pounds at a time, which they'd typically stash in the bottom of a boat and then attach to their legs with rope before swimming ashore. Meanwhile, they'd formed their own commune in San Diego called "the Family," and had hooked up with the Brotherhood of Eternal Love, a group of hippies and surfers living in cheap houses in Laguna Beach who were smuggling untold quantities of hashish from Afghanistan and transporting massive quantities of Mexican weed across the border.

Smuggling and selling hash and marijuana became a way for the Family, the Brotherhood, and legions of other hippies to finance their alternative lifestyles. As more young people started tuning in, turning on, and dropping out, the demand for Mexican buds grew even higher, and Hoxter was often handling shipments of one thousand or one thousand five hundred pounds at a time. Because of the volume they handled, the various drug networks operating at the time soon had no use for Tijuana middlemen and had hooked up directly with individual villages in the Mexican states of Sinaloa, Jalisco, or Michoacan, where growing marijuana had long been a way of life. The Family patronized one particular hamlet high up in the hills of Michoacan, an hour or so south of Morelia. After a decade of cross-border enterprise, the jungle township had doubled in size and enjoyed electricity, plumbing, and paved roads.

When Southern California got too crowded—and too hot— Hoxter and the Family moved to rural Montana, and Hoxter began a new life smuggling Mexican loads across the border into Canada. His first crossing was insanely risky: he drove through a one-man border control checkpoint with his Canuck girlfriend, posing as newlyweds. "My chances were probably 80-20 that I'd get caught,"

Hoxter estimates. "But I told her to look at this guy and melt him. I want him to think if I wasn't sitting here, he'd had a shot with you."

Hoxter's girlfriend was a stunner, and the happy couple was soon in Vancouver unloading four hundred pounds of pot, which is how Hoxter met a friend of a friend nicknamed Art Nouveau, who became his partner in crime for the next twenty-five years. Thanks to his connections in Vancouver, a group of hippies who were the biggest pot dealers in British Columbia, Hoxter was never short of work when it came to smuggling weed. He spent most of the 1970s living off the grid at the Family's commune in Montana, raising chickens and pigs and running pot across the border, one thousand pounds at a time. Every month a truck would come from Southern California, full of marijuana from Mexico. Hoxter had a collection of US Forestry Service topographical maps, and knew all the unused service roads that led to the Canadian border.

"On the maps, the roads ended at the border, but you knew they didn't really end but went straight into Canada," he explains. "All you had to do was choose one that would dump you out close to a paved road, because once you were on the pavement you could be anybody, even if you did have Montana plates, which was okay." While driving through people's farms on the way to the main road, Hoxter says, nobody seemed to mind as long as he remembered to shut their gates so their cows wouldn't wander off. Often Hoxter would drive close enough to a farmhouse to actually see a farmer and his wife sitting at their dinner table, making eye contact with him in that subtle country manner. Not once did he forget to close a gate, nor did he ever cross paths with the Canadian border patrol.

A growing stack of bills from each successful sojourn, stashed in a hole in the ground under one of the houses, funded the Family's hardscrabble existence. If someone needed money to travel somewhere or buy groceries or supplies, Hoxter, who was known among members of the commune as "Controller," would simply disburse the cash on a case-by-case basis, using larger amounts to finance ever-larger marijuana shipments that were always being orchestrated either via the Brotherhood or directly from Mexico. The biggest Mexican load Hoxter ever handled was a seaborne haul, three-tons of a five-ton deal, put together with his friends in the Brotherhood, who provided a yacht to transport the weed from Mexico. But the pot almost never reached its destination, because the yacht broke down.

"The price for losing that load was our lives," Hoxter recalls, his voice suddenly catching in his throat. "The Mexicans would have killed us if we lost it." In fact, one of the crewmembers did lose his life, but that was before the boat broke its driveline. "One of the San Diego kids fell overboard on the trip north," Hoxter says. "I don't know how it happened. You're out there in the deep blue; it was nighttime. The captain said, 'We're not turning around. Sorry, but your friend is gone.'"

Hoxter had no choice but to fly back north, inform his friend's parents that their son had died in a sailing accident, and then raise $33,000 to buy the spare parts for the boat, which sat useless in a Pacific Ocean port. Finally, he had to convince his girlfriend to let him strap her down with the cash, which he carefully wrapped around her torso after instructing her to look everyone in the eye and, when necessary, to flirt. Then he purchased airline tickets to fly her and her husband—yes, his girlfriend had a husband; this was the early 1970s after all—down to Mexico. The couple posed as newlyweds on honeymoon, and once they arrived in Mexico City, Hoxter's contacts delivered the money to the port where the boat was waiting. After the cash arrived, the parts were purchased and the load miraculously arrived a few weeks later at an isolated beach on the US Marine Corps base in Camp Pendleton. The spot was accessible by a dirt road and guarded only by a chain-link gate secured with a padlock. Hoxter and his cohorts used inflatable motorized rafts to run the bundles of marijuana off the yacht onto the beach; the haul filled up two Winnebago motor homes which Hoxter purchased, cash down, just to transport the goods.

Because the trip had taken a few months longer than projected, Hoxter ended up owing the Brotherhood some money, and to pay them off, he had no choice but to make a one-thousand-pound run to Canada. Usually, that was no problem. However, now it was the dead of winter and fourteen feet of snow blanketed the border between Montana and Canada. The Forest Service had also blown up some of the decrepit bridges Hoxter had been using to run drugs, and had even constructed giant earthen berms along the roads to prevent all but the foolhardiest four-wheel-drivers from attempting passage. Hoxter's solution, hitching trailers loaded with pot to a pair of snowmobiles, seemed to work until halfway up the mountain, when one of them busted a fan belt from the strain of carrying the heavy load.

He and his friend were able to weave the belt back together with some spare wire before they froze to death, but the mission was over. The next night, Hoxter waited until long after sunset and walked up to a border checkpoint that was only open during the daytime. He yelled and cursed at the top of his lungs and smashed a couple of bottles of tequila on the road. "Nobody came out," he says. "So the next night, I went up to the gate and cut the lock with bolt cutters at 3:00 AM." On cue, Hoxter's friend, behind the wheel of a truck with the pot, roared through the checkpoint. An hour later, they unloaded the weed, and were back through the border before anyone knew the gate's lock had been broken.

In the early 1980s—Hoxter can't remember the exact year—the Family commune in Montana began to fall apart under the strain of cabin fever and rapidly approaching middle age, and he and his wife moved to Lebanon, Oregon. There, they raised three daughters on a 2,500-acre property. They lived in a small trailer, but not because the property lacked proper shelter. In fact, Hoxter had purchased the land because it featured a large barn, which he had every intention of using for growing marijuana. Inside the barn, Hoxter wired together several one-thousand-watt metal-halide lamps, hanging them from the beams, and reflected the heat with Mylar sheeting in a ten-by-twelve-foot enclosure. When the female plants reached a certain height, he moved them to various locations he'd scouted in nearby national forest land where, if he could keep the herb stalks hidden long enough, he could harvest his cannabis crop before the feds ripped them from the soil.

This being the dawn of the homegrown American marijuana farming industry, Hoxter was hardly the only hippie in rural Oregon who had his own pot farm. There wasn't much else to do. The logging industry had been on the wane for years, and unemployment ran high in the small towns. "All I wanted to do was grow, although Canada was always my ace in the hole," Hoxter says. "I knew that I could always make a lot of money smuggling a load. At first, I was the only person I knew growing indoor with lights. But then a friend of mine started growing, and he used sodium-vapor lights, which turned out to have a better light spectrum for growing, and this kind of information would get spread like that." There was even a local magazine for growers called *Sinsemilla Tips* that passed along word-of-mouth horticultural advice. "People were learning," Hoxter says. "There were still no names for the product yet, none of the strains had been branded, and botanists were just starting to figure out how to crossbreed hybrids. It was all still just marijuana."

Every night, the local television station would broadcast reports on how many plants the feds had spotted with their planes and seized in the forests that day. But Hoxter never was caught, and everything went just like he'd hoped, until his wife became ill and died in 1987. Thus began a downward spiral for Hoxter. Or rather, thus ended a downward spiral that had already begun well before his wife died, one which had been amplified by the highly illegal nature of everything he'd been doing for the past few decades. His career ended with him becoming mentally and physically isolated, alone with three daughters, unable to cope, strung out on heroin, and dealing harder drugs to support his habit. Just when things couldn't get any worse, the feds raided his farm.

After a stint in federal prison, Hoxter relocated to Southern California, where he went straight back into the marijuana business. But a cop in Laguna Beach who knew of his background as a smuggler got wind of his presence there and raided his house six times in ten months, until on the last raid, he caught Hoxter with a couple of pounds of weed, enough to charge him with possession with the intent to sell. Hoxter served the next forty-one months in federal lockup, and came out determined to put his criminal escapades behind him, although he reserved the right to smoke marijuana.

"I was on parole and had eighteen dirty tests in a row," he explains. "My parole officer could have sent me back to prison, but she didn't, because I was working full-time, and for some reason, she liked me. "Fifty years ago you could go to prison for drinking beer and now you can do that legally," Hoxter told her. "So was it wrong then?"

"I'm not going to argue with you," the parole officer responded. "But it's against the law and you don't seem to get it."

Except that marijuana wasn't illegal any more.

Not *exactly*, that is.

— — — — —

Just weeks after the last time Hoxter was busted for marijuana, in November 1996, California voters overwhelmingly voted in favor of Proposition 215, which legalized marijuana for medical purposes under state law for the first time in American history. The law was written by a group of marijuana-legalization activists in the Bay Area, most notably a San Francisco resident named Dennis Peron whose partner had used cannabis to treat the symptoms of his AIDS virus before he passed away from the disease. According to the new law, which became known as the Compassionate Use Act, if a doctor wrote a recommendation—not a prescription, since it remained illegal for doctors to prescribe—for marijuana, a patient could grow, possess, and smoke the substance with no fear of the law. In the wake of that vote, activists up and down the state began forming collectives to provide marijuana to members, openly announcing their intentions at city council meetings and in letters to politicians and police departments. They'd soon regret being so foolish. Two of the activists who jumped on the medical marijuana bandwagon too fast and too soon were Martin Chavez and David Herrick. They were among the first victims of the statewide law enforcement crackdown that followed the passage of Prop. 215.

I followed both of their cases as a reporter for *OC Weekly*, Orange County's alternative newsweekly, where I now work as a managing editor, and in 1999, the newsweekly nominated Chavez as "Man of the Year" in celebration of his efforts to provide medical marijuana to low-income patients—much to his own peril. Chavez grew up in the industrial, working-class barrio of Huntington Park, California. In 1972, when he was just seventeen, Chavez dropped out of high school. He begged his mother to sign paperwork allowing him to join the Marine Corps Reserve before his eighteenth birthday. She did, and Chavez served in the corps for the next six years. In his spare time, he worked construction jobs and ultimately went into business for himself as a small contractor. He married, fathered two children, and developed a bad habit: cocaine. In 1991, Chavez was convicted of possession and sent to Tehachapi state prison for two years.

Determined to get his life on track, Chavez participated in a work-furlough program. While being transported with several other inmates to a work site, Chavez suffered a back injury when the van he was in struck a parked Jeep. Chavez was transferred to the state prison in Chino, where he worked in the dining room. Mopping the floor one day in 1992, Chavez slipped and injured his back once again. Unable to walk or stand straight, he was finally given some pills and a back brace before being released from prison the next year. Free once again, Chavez found himself in constant pain. Worse, the medication he had been prescribed was turning him into a zombie. He didn't just feel no pain; he felt nothing at all and was incapable of even leaving the house. "The medication made me a hermit," he remembers. "I had mood swings. I didn't want to communicate with my sons. The side effects were too hard on me. I didn't want to be around people."

He went to a doctor who ran a blood test and made the startling discovery that Chavez was suffering the onset of a genetically inherited spinal condition that can sometimes be triggered by back trauma. The disease, ankylosing spondylitis, inevitably fuses together the victim's bones until complete paralysis takes over. It's a process that is as excruciatingly painful as it sounds. From visits to a public library and through appointments with local doctors, Chavez learned that many in the medical community saw marijuana as a safer, healthier painkiller and appetite-inducer than several of the medications he was already taking.

After Proposition 215 became law, Chavez, who was then living in the Disneyland-adjacent suburb of Garden Grove, decided to set up a nonprofit cannabis co-op, the Orange County Cannabis Patient-Doctor-Nurse Support Group. His goal was to make marijuana available to sick people on fixed incomes who were unable to grow it themselves. If Chavez was a drug dealer, he was an inept one. In late 1996, just weeks after Prop. 215's passage, he spoke with Garden Grove city officials, announcing his intention to open the co-op. He pleaded fruitlessly with the city elders for permission to set up an office somewhere in the city and wrote letters to then–Orange County Sheriff Brad Gates expressing his hope that the county's law enforcement folks would work with him to ensure that the co-op would remain on the good side of the law. He religiously advertised his efforts in the local media, expanding on his vision with any reporter who would listen.

The press interviews, the city hall speechifying, the letters: it was an odd campaign for someone allegedly trying to run a criminal drug operation. But that's exactly what authorities said Chavez and his friend David Herrick, a former San Bernardino County sheriff's deputy, were trying to do when they arrested Chavez in January 1998. Police had already arrested Herrick at a hotel room a few months earlier, confiscating several sandwich-sized bags of marijuana marked NOT FOR SALE, FOR MEDICAL USE ONLY. The cops also found a database of the club's membership, which led them to two members: one who suffered from chronic back pain and another carrying a card identifying him as the caregiver for a lung cancer patient who was the ultimate recipient of the marijuana.

The prosecutor who tried Herrick in court for four counts of selling marijuana was Carl Armbrust, an octogenarian Eliot Ness who'd been with the DA's office so long that he'd helped take down the Brotherhood of Eternal Love when it fell victim to an Orange County grand jury investigation and multi-agency drug task force back in 1972. Armbrust's dislike for marijuana hadn't softened just because of some silly vote by the people of California. As far as he was concerned, marijuana was still illegal under federal law and people like Herrick and Chavez were just dope dealers. When I asked him whether or not he disputed the medicinal qualities of marijuana as far as treating pain, Armbrust chuckled. "Sure marijuana makes you feel great," he answered. "So does drinking a glass of scotch. That's why they call it getting high."

Armbrust sent Chavez a subpoena to appear at Herrick's trial; the two shook each other's hands, and then a few days later, investigators working for Armbrust busted Chavez for providing marijuana to an undercover officer posing as a sick patient. Chavez wound up in state prison for more than a year. Meanwhile, in Herrick's trial, the courtroom proceedings at time resembled a scene from *Alice in Wonderland*. During one particularly weird moment, Armbrust became visibly upset when one of Herrick's medical marijuana customers failed to answer a subpoena demanding he appear in court to testify against Herrick. Suspecting the customer had friends in the courtroom, he threatened to have the would-be witness arrested but withdrew the threat when he learned the man was bedridden at a hospice, dying a slow and painful death.

Not once during his trial was Herrick allowed to mention the words "medical marijuana." Nor was he able to tell the jury how he first discovered its benefits in Vietnam circa 1969, when he was a combat medic assigned to the First Air Cavalry Division in the Central Highlands. Herrick volunteered for duty through the buddy system; his best friend worked on a medevac chopper and died six months after arriving in country. Herrick survived numerous firefights with the North Vietnamese Army, many of them bloody battles over remote hilltops that the Americans abandoned as soon as they captured them.

"Guys were dying, losing legs, and everyone was getting hooked on heroin," Herrick later told me. "The junkies in my company would raid my morphine whenever they couldn't get their heroin. No matter where I put it, in my aid bag or in the front pocket of my fatigues or even if I tried to bury it in the bottom of the rucksack— it'd always end up gone." About a month into Herrick's tour, his company was patrolling a rubber plantation outside Tay Ninh when it took small-arms fire from a band of Viet Cong. A soldier standing next to Herrick, who'd just arrived four days ago, took a bullet in the shoulder and fell to the ground.

"This kid was eighteen years old and scared shitless," Herrick recalled. "He was sobbing like a banshee. I had no morphine. So I went over to a guy I knew who had just scored and grabbed two joints and gave them to the kid. He fired one up." Herrick busied himself treating other wounded soldiers. Five minutes later, he checked back in on the kid. "He was lying against a tree," Herrick said, "joking like it was no big thing."

From then on, whenever he could, Herrick would medicate wounded soldiers with marijuana, a habit that won him a shouting match with his commanding officer, who felt the drug would render his soldiers useless and worried the smell would attract the enemy. Herrick argued that a wounded infantryman who was screaming his lungs out posed a worse problem than a stoned grunt who shut up and stayed out of the way. The two men locked horns for twenty minutes before his commanding officer backed down.

Herrick made a particularly unlikely target for the likes of Armbrust. After returning from the war a decorated hero, Herrick became a San Bernardino County Sheriff's Deputy, which is how he became a medical marijuana patient. In 1991, after fifteen years on the job, Herrick's patrol car ran over him while he was getting out of the driver's seat during a routine traffic stop. "As I was getting out of the car, it shifted from park to reverse, caught my leg, and pulled me under," Herrick explained. "It took out my disc and herniated it so bad that it was irreparable."

After three months in bed, where he was prescribed a regimen of Vicodin, Percodan, and codeine, Herrick realized he was addicted to the medications. His doctor told him that if it were legal for him to do so, he'd gladly write him a pain-relief prescription for cannabis.

Herrick tried it and was sold; he even helped gather signatures in support of Prop. 215, which is how he befriended and ultimately went into business with Chavez.

For his crimes, Herrick went to prison for twenty-nine months, until the California Court of Appeals ruled that Armbrust had committed prosecutorial misconduct by misleading the jury about the evidence against Herrick during his closing remarks.

"Do you want to know why I did twenty-nine months in prison?" Herrick asked me, not long after his release. "For furnishing three-quarters of an ounce of marijuana to a man who had a doctor's written recommendation and was dying of terminal lung cancer."

— — — — —

Flash forward fifteen years to the summer of 2011, which is starting to look a lot like the historical high-water mark of the medical marijuana movement, although few realized it at the time. Besides California, fifteen other states—Arizona, Alaska, Montana, Colorado, and Nevada among them—as well as the District of Columbia have passed laws legalizing medical marijuana. Cannabis is California's biggest cash crop, with an annual harvest valued at about $14 billion. With an estimated annual yield of 8.6 million pounds, it represents by far the largest share of the national cannabis crop, which itself is valued at $35 billion.

It's estimated that as much as $1.4 billion worth of cannabis is sold each year in California. Because state law views medical marijuana as a medicine, some dispensaries have gone to court to avoid paying sales tax, arguing that cannabis should be exempt from it like any other prescribed medicine. However, as of 2011, the California State Board of Equalization estimated that it was taking in between $58 million and $105 million a year in taxes on cannabis sales. In 2010, the city of Oakland, with its four mega-dispensaries, including the world-famous Oaksterdam University—founded by the wheelchair-bound, bespectacled ex-roadie Richard Lee and which has its own nursery and has provided cultivation classes to thousands of activists—and Stephen DeAngelo's Harborside Health Center—the subject of the Discovery Channel reality show *Weed Wars*, which aired in 2011—collected $1 million in tax revenue.

Starting in the mid-2000s, meanwhile, hundreds of medical cannabis dispensaries had opened up throughout the state, mostly in densely populated urban neighborhoods of cities such as San Francisco and Los Angeles, spreading from there to the suburbs. For as little as fifty dollars, a California resident could drop by a doctor's office—some of them conveniently located next-door to dispensaries—and obtain a written recommendation for marijuana. With that in hand you could walk into your dispensary of choice and after signing membership paperwork, you could select your "medicine" from row upon row of various strains of cannabis indica and sativa with sometimes exotic but more often recreational-sounding names such as Hindu Kush, Chem Dog, Luke Skywalker, Sweet Tooth, and Sour Diesel.

Meanwhile, local prosecutors in states that have legalized marijuana for medical use now refuse to file charges against anyone with a doctor's note as long as they aren't transporting or cultivating more weed than what is allowed under state law—usually half a dozen fully grown plants or up to eight ounces of dry marijuana. Knowing this, assuming the person has a valid doctor's note, it's likely the police won't even confiscate the cannabis in question. It's now just an infraction—the legal equivalent of a parking ticket—to possess an ounce or less of the stuff—and that's assuming you're the rare recreational pot smoker who's too lazy to get a doctor's note. Oaksterdam's Lee even paid $1.5 million to sponsor a law, Prop. 19, that would have legalized the recreational use of marijuana for adults, but it failed at the polls in November 2010.

Since the first anti-cannabis law was enacted by the Massachusetts state legislature on April 29, 1911, pot smokers have blossomed from a handful of jazz musicians to tens of millions of people. Some twenty million Americans have been arrested on marijuana charges so far, and forty thousand people remain behind bars for marijuana-related crimes. And just as marijuana seemed poised to become completely legal in California, thus providing possible impetus to a nationwide campaign of decriminalization, everything changed. In October 2011, the federal government began a massive crackdown on California's medical marijuana industry, raiding dispensaries up and down the coast, seizing property from landlords who were renting to people growing or distributing pot, and hitting DeAngelo's Harborside—the nation's largest dispensary with more than ninety thousand members—with a $2.4 million tax bill, while also pressuring the dispensary's landlord to evict. Oaksterdam was next. On April 2, 2012, federal drug agents backed by local police raided the university in downtown Oakland, as well as Lee's house, and seized his entire nursery; Lee announced a few days later that he was giving up the medical marijuana business.

The raids continued throughout 2012, with particular intensity in places where local officials had grown fed up with large numbers of dispensaries, like Los Angeles, Orange County, and especially Long Beach, which as this book will reveal, engaged in a mercurial experiment with medical marijuana that will likely remain unrivaled in its hypocrisy in the annals of drug policy. Within the space of two years, the city invited cannabis clubs to pay tens of thousands of dollars to apply to win city approval, wrote an elaborate city ordinance mandating the cultivation of marijuana within city limits, engaged in a suspicious and sloppy lottery process to award clubs that had met the criteria, and then refused to provide any club with a permit. Meanwhile, the city frequently raided the clubs that had smartly avoided the lottery fiasco. Lawsuits by cannabis patients and dispensaries against the city were filed as a result; taken together they could bankrupt Long Beach.

By the eve of the US Presidential Election in November 2012, it seemed official: the medical marijuana movement had reached its apex. The movement had failed. The industry that had boomed in the past three years was doomed to decline. And then on Election Day, voters in Washington State and Colorado passed state laws legalizing marijuana for recreational use, something that had been attempted more than once in California, most recently in 2009, but which had never won at the polls. A cover story in *Newsweek* magazine just weeks before the Colorado measure passed shed light on the corporate backers of the legalization measure, dubbing them America's new "pot barons." Just as the federal government's successful takedown of California's dispensaries showed the abject failure of medical marijuana to protect both the crop and the people growing it, American democracy had stepped in and provided new hope for stoners.

This book is about a relatively brief time but amazing period in American social history—an incredibly dynamic three years from 2009 to 2012 during which something unprecedented happened— marijuana left the underground world of illegality and blossomed into a mainstream industry, becoming the fastest-growing economic engine in California before the feds swooped in and put pot back in its "proper" place.

The weed runners who inhabit this book are pioneers of the future American pot economy, whatever form it ultimately takes. Some of them are martyrs who paved the way for the explosion of medical marijuana. They lost their liberty by trying to accomplish too much too soon. Others followed in their footsteps, some more cautiously than others, risking everything including their own freedom to push the limits of this grand experiment.

As the book reveals, some weed runners have better intentions than others, and the well-intentioned ironically have tended to suffer worse fates at the hands of the law for their efforts. Some are smarter or just luckier than others, too. Generally speaking, these outlaw capitalists are the weed runners who have decidedly remained in the underground pot economy, or at least kept part of their portfolio firmly rooted in America's illicit pot trade. They view themselves as the next Jamesons and Johnnie Walkers. They are modern-day bootleggers who have helped lay the nationwide foundation for the brand-name marijuana of today and tomorrow. For them, the medical marijuana industry, and the war to curtail it, is just a sideshow. They know that until full legalization occurs, the real profits from pot will come from one source: smuggling weed across the country the good old-fashioned way. Regardless of the debate over medical marijuana, and certainly without regard for the law, they will be meeting America's incessant demand for weed one high-risk shipment at a time.

1 | Racer X

Yoga Girl has just woken up from a nap.

The smile on her face suggests it's postcoital. Slender and pale with an upturned nose, she has long, curly hair swept over her shoulder. She wears a pair of tight yoga-style gray sweatpants and an indigo-colored top. Her boyfriend, who is shirtless with black slacks, is a handsome, tanned teenager with a slicked-back blond mane and an uncanny resemblance to Leonardo DiCaprio.

Yoga Girl is a college freshman from Los Angeles who grew up in Newport Beach and has just moved back home for the summer, renting an apartment a few blocks from the beach. She's counting out twenty dollar bills on a coffee table while her boyfriend stretches out on a futon.

"Here you go," she says. "That's my ID card. Do you have change for $200?"

Standing next to the coffee table is someone I've known for years who prefers, for the purposes of this book, to be identified only as "Racer X."

He's a short, wiry surfer with a crew cut, tattoos on his arms, and a briefcase full of manila envelopes, each of which contains from one to six airtight, plastic containers full of medical marijuana. The girl has just shown him her State of California Medical Marijuana Identification Card (she'd read her ID number to Racer X's boss over the phone an hour or so earlier), and Racer X has just handed her an envelope containing a quarter-ounce of pot, half of which is Lavender Kush—at seventy-five dollars per eighth, one of the luxury strains available to medical marijuana smokers—and half of which is Northern Kush, which is also seventy-five dollars per eighth-ounce.

Racer X is a part-time driver for one of some two dozen cannabis clubs in Orange County that offer members door-to-door marijuana delivery services. His day job involves stocking groceries at a local supermarket chain. He's been a recreational marijuana smoker for years, typically toking up early in the morning before hitting the waves on his days off or in the evenings after work. He bought his pot from a dealer and fellow surfer whom we'll call "the Big Kahuna."

For years, the Big Kahuna had made a decent living selling pot to customers such as Racer X. But as his client base aged, got married, had kids, and smoked less weed, he began to worry about finding a real job. It didn't help that hundreds of marijuana dispensaries had since opened their doors in Los Angeles, offering high-quality marijuana to anyone with a doctor's note. After the Orange County Board of Supervisors, following several similar votes by their colleagues elsewhere around the state, voted in July 2007 to allow county residents to apply for state medical-marijuana ID cards, the Big Kahuna formed a legally registered nonprofit cooperative that would supply medical marijuana to members of the "club." He attended classes held by the California branch of the National Organization for the Reform of Marijuana Laws (better known by its acronym, NORML) and learned how to operate within the somewhat fuzzy boundaries established in state law for the operation of such collectives.

The Big Kahuna created a website for his club—the name of which he asked not to be revealed—and advertised on various marijuana websites, such as www.weedmaps.com and www.weedtracker.com; Yoga Girl found the club through one of the two sites.

"I think it was Weedmaps," she says.

"We just looked for the closest one in our ZIP code," her boyfriend chimes in.

"Yeah, that's how we found you," says Yoga Girl, who adds that she discovered Weedmaps through her sorority sisters in Los Angeles. There was a cannabis dispensary conveniently located down the street from her dormitory. "Now that I'm down here for the summer, I didn't want to drive up to L.A.," she says. "For safety reasons, too. If you have enough money for a card, having it delivered to you is definitely the way to go. You know, why not?"

I ask her what symptom she has that allows her to smoke marijuana. Yoga Girl pauses for a moment. "Uh, migraines?" she finally ventures. "I use it as a, um, sleep aid. Yeah."

"Does it work?" I ask.

"Oh, yeah; yeah, it does," she says, giggling.

Racer X laughs with delight as he zips up his briefcase and nods at the door. He's in a rush to make it to his next delivery on schedule.

"Oh, yeah," Racer X exclaims, waving good-bye to Yoga Girl. "Weed works, baby!"

─ ─ ─ ─ ─

An hour earlier on this breezy summer day in 2009, I'm sitting with Racer X and the Big Kahuna in a small room inside a two-bedroom house in Newport Beach. It's the Big Kahuna's home office, headquarters of his six-year-old cannabis club, which he opened up to new members in November 2008. An American flag hangs on the wall, and stacks of large, airtight plastic bins fill one of the room's corners, all of them stuffed with one of nineteen strains of marijuana with gloriously hyperbolic handles and descriptions such as Skywalker (a "tractor beam to Super Spacey!") and Sour Diesel ("Good luck shutting up; Ramble alert!"). Two computers, one of which is cranking alternative rock via Pandora, a free online music station, take up a wraparound desk in another corner of the room. Several open containers of marijuana lay on the few available flat surfaces.

As usual, the Big Kahuna is sitting shirtless in his chair, flexing his large forearms around a giant glass bong. He takes a deep hit from the device and exhales powerfully into a one-inch-thick plastic tube that he has rigged to a spot in the wall near an air-conditioning unit. "That stuff can go outside," he explains, nodding at the smoke. "I don't care. It's legal."

Just then, his cell phone rings. The Big Kahuna spends the next twenty minutes explaining the various benefits of different strains of marijuana to a repeat customer who agrees to buy a quarter-ounce of a sativa strain. "There are two major groups of cannabis: indica and sativa," he tells me after hanging up. "Most of the weed coming into California and being grown in California in the past twenty years was all indica because people wanted to get stoned and sit on the couch. But if you give that indica to patients who are in pain, in misery, already in a bad place, it takes them down and makes them depressed and suicidal. Sativa is an upper, like coffee. It kills the pain and leaves the patient awake and aware and motivated instead of mellow."

The person who just called has ordered a few eighths of a sativa strain, the Big Kahuna explains. "This guy has a metal rod inserted in his back, and it's fused to his spine. He's been on painkillers for ten years and is trying to get off them. He's a regular customer.

This is his third or fourth time. He orders from us every couple of weeks."

A former pot dealer who spent time in jail after being set up by a large-scale pot mover who turned out to be an informant for the local police department of this affluent coastal suburban town, the Big Kahuna is an expert in what is legal and what is not so legal when it comes to medical marijuana. He's determined to stay on the legal side of things—unlike, he asserts, the hundreds of L.A. cannabis dispensaries that have opened in the past several years, many of which have been subjected to raids by both state and federal law-enforcement authorities.

"These dispensaries offer everything," he explains. "Food, drink, tinctures, concentrates like hashish, and all that stuff isn't outlined in the law."

The law in question, State Bill 420, which was enacted in 2008 to regulate medical marijuana, only allows dispensaries and clubs to grow and provide to their members dried cannabis. For that reason, the Big Kahuna tells me, he can only obtain marijuana from members of his club, all of whom must live in Orange County. He can't buy pot from growers, say, in Los Angeles or Northern California. He can deliver the locally grown pot to as many members of the club who live in Orange County as he wishes, so long as he has each member sign a form designating him as their primary caregiver. According to California NORML, there are nearly 150 delivery services throughout the state, most of them in the Bay Area and Los Angeles.

The Big Kahuna tells me that the big L.A. dispensaries are also delivering marijuana to customers in Orange County, despite SB420 stating that designated caregivers can't cross county lines. "It's the Wild West up in L.A.," he complains. "They are getting busted because they are bringing five pounds of weed in the back door and selling it out the front door, whereas we don't do more than an ounce, which is what a [single] person could truly consume." While the Big Kahuna acknowledges that half of his club's members "just want to get high," he says the other half is made up of legitimate patients.

– – – – –

Racer X is driving a beat-up truck with a satellite-powered global-positioning device mounted on his dashboard. The GPS beeps every few seconds and provides a constant stream of directions. "Turn right, then turn left," it might say, or "Now arriving at destination." When Racer X misses a turn, usually because he's too busy talking, the machine alerts him to his error with the word "Recalculating." "That's the last word I want to hear," he says. That word means he's getting lost and losing time, and time is money.

He delivers weed for the Big Kahuna three days a week, in shifts that last from 3:00 to 8:00 PM. His busiest days are Fridays, when he can make as many as eight deliveries and earn up to $200. For each eighth of an ounce he delivers, Racer X earns a $10 commission. Sometimes, people tip him $20. Once, a pretty girl ran after him with a twenty dollar bill that he'd mistakenly given her when counting out her change. "This is yours," she said. "I was going to keep it, but you're the last person I want to piss off."

Today, Racer X is eager to stay on schedule because a few days earlier, he missed an entire shift—seven deliveries, a lot for a Wednesday—because the springs in his garage door broke and he couldn't move his truck. He's grateful that we reach the day's first customer—the man with the metal rod in his back—in just a few minutes.

Unlike Yoga Girl, this customer isn't willing to be interviewed on tape. He happily takes off his Hawaiian shirt to reveal a back brace, which he also removes. A nasty scar stretches from the nape of his neck to his tailbone; another traces a curve along the left side of his ribcage. He broke his back on the job several years ago and is trying to kick an Oxycontin addiction. He smokes marijuana to relieve the constant pain in his back. It relaxes him enough that he can play his guitar. He's clearly lonely; for someone who doesn't want to be interviewed, he has a lot to say. He follows Racer X all the way to his truck in the parking lot of the condominium complex and reluctantly waves good-bye.

Next, Racer X delivers half an ounce of weed to a weathered, middle-aged Latino man who is cooking chicken in his Costa Mesa apartment and watching a Lakers game. "You guys want some food?" he asks, but Racer X is eager to move on. He's got one more delivery to make back in Newport Beach. Then his cell phone rings. It's the Big Kahuna, telling Racer X that the last customer of the night is about to leave for dinner. Racer X can't make it to the house in time, so the Big Kahuna agrees to make this delivery, since he's closer. "Next time, drop off at the houses that are close by first," the Big Kahuna says. When Racer X tries to protest, the Big Kahuna cuts him short. "I'm the chief, and you're the Indian," he says. "Got it?"

– – – – –

A week later, on another Friday afternoon, I join Racer X again. After meeting at the Big Kahuna's house to pick up several manila envelopes for the first few deliveries of the shift, we drive to an apartment complex just five minutes away in Newport Beach. The only problem: the apartment is on a street that Racer X's talking GPS device doesn't recognize. It keeps telling him how to reach a street with a similar name. Ten confusing minutes and a few dozen screamed epithets later, Racer X finally finds the complex. He calls the customer's telephone number three times, but nobody answers. Finally, Racer X realizes he was calling the wrong number.

After being buzzed in, we walk into the dimly lit apartment of a fat man watching Fox News. A diploma on the wall identifies him as a doctor of philosophy. He buys a quarter-ounce of weed. The next delivery is to someone who lives in Huntington Beach. Because Interstate 405 is jammed with traffic, we take surface streets, which turn out to be just as congested. (Racer X will later realize that with me in the car, we could have taken the carpool lane.)

At just after 5:00 PM on a Friday night—the worst time for rush-hour traffic in coastal Orange County—Racer X starts to lose his patience. Despite having medicated himself with marijuana earlier in the day, he's exhibiting clear symptoms of road rage.

"Come on, dude!" he yells at a driver who fails to notice the traffic light change from red to green. "You don't have to go home, but you can't stay here!"

Finally, the driver begins to roll forward, and Racer X breathes a deep sigh of relief. "Sometimes, I feel like a taxi driver," he says. "I've learned how to dodge around in traffic and avoid the really bad intersections so I don't lose too much time. But I've also learned how to calm myself down while driving. I need to be able to do that because I'm driving around in a car full of something that is still considered a banned substance under federal law, and I don't want to draw any more attention to myself than I need to."

It's clear that despite, or perhaps because of, the fact that Racer X medicates himself with copious amounts of marijuana on a daily basis, he's a pretty paranoid individual. Driving around stoned with packages of weed in a suitcase in his backseat all day long, after all, isn't exactly a risk-free activity, even if there are literally dozens of delivery services and hundreds of drivers just like Racer X doing that exact thing—except for maybe the driving-while-stoned part.

There's always the possibility of being pulled over by the cops, who will not look kindly on all those eighth-ounce containers of marijuana—clear evidence, they could argue, that Racer X is in possession of pot with the intent to sell, a serious felony that could lead to months if not years in jail. Racer X's proximity sense seems to escalate as we approach the city of Huntington Beach, which has more police cruisers prowling the streets per capita than anyplace else in his delivery area. His eyes continuously flick upward to his rearview mirror.

As we reach the neighborhood where the next customer lives, a strange slice of suburbia where all the houses are built in a faux half-timber Tudor-era style, Racer X is busy explaining how he's learned to identify prostitutes. "You can tell that's what they are because they're always sitting at the bus stop, but they never get on a bus," he says.

"Sometimes, it really pisses me off," he continues. "Once I saw this Mexican lady with a kid sitting on the bench waiting for the bus, and four hours later, she was still there. I just don't get it."

Suddenly, Racer X's GPS device interrupts his rant. "Recalculating," it says. "Recalculating . . . Recalculating."

Racer X has missed his left turn. "You have got to be kidding me!" he shouts. "How the fuck do I make a U-turn?"

— — — — —

At first glance, the Serial Killer looks like any other young Southern California skate punk, except he's wearing mirrored sunglasses inside his tiny, cramped apartment. The glasses, combined with his wool hat and leering smile, make him look like Richard Ramirez, the infamous Night Stalker. The only thing scarier than him is his dog, which is about twice his size. The animal looks like the kind of Belgian attack dog the South African police might have used to terrify anti-apartheid protesters at the height of the township rebellions; it's trying to push down a sliding patio door and eat Racer X.

This is Racer X's second delivery to the Serial Killer in just two weeks—that's when the Serial Killer moved to this unit—and he's already buying another five-eighths of an ounce of weed. Today's transaction takes less than a minute. "Thanks," the Serial Killer says. "I won't be here next time, just so you know. I'm moving." A few minutes later, Racer X gets a call from the Big Kahuna, who tells him that several more orders have just come in. "We're going to head back and do a pick-up-and-fly-by," Racer X tells me.

We drive back to the Big Kahuna's house. He walks out to the truck and hands over several manila envelopes. Seconds later, we're on our way to meet the next customer, a friendly but serious young man who lives in a surreal-looking neighborhood of Huntington Beach where all the houses resemble blown-up versions of structures you'd find at a miniature-golf course, minus the windmills. He says he works for a surgical-supply company and smokes medical marijuana to soothe his tension headaches, which he'd been diagnosed with as a teenager. He buys an eighth of an ounce of weed.

"I've had these headaches since high school," he says. "I've taken Tylenol and other over-the-counter drugs, but I really don't like them. I smoke this a couple of times a month," he adds, pointing at the just-purchased marijuana. "I mean, this will last me quite a long time, quite frankly."

The next customer is Racer X's favorite client. As we drive to meet her, he regales me with tales of her physical attributes. "She's, like, six-three, six-four, big-boned, and beautiful, like a Nordic Amazon warrior," he enthuses. "She says she has a boyfriend, but she's really friendly."

We pull up to the luxury condominium complex where the girl lives. A few minutes later, she bounds down the street and marches up to the truck with a happy grin on her face and leans in the driver's window.

"Hiya!" she says.

Racer X is in love.

The Nordic Amazon warrior, who is about a foot shorter and several dress sizes larger than Racer X had claimed, is really happy to see him. She freely acknowledges that her diagnosed medical condition—anxiety—is just a ruse to get high without breaking the law. She explains that she grew up on the East Coast and recounts horror stories about trying to find weed. "I remember the hunts we used to go on back home," she says. "It would be hours and hours and twenty or thirty phone calls before you'd get lucky. Hmmm: yeah, anxiety," she adds, laughing at the memories. "Not anymore!"

— — — — —

The final delivery of the day takes place in a parking lot near a Petco. For some reason, this customer always insists on meeting in that lot, something that troubles Racer X. "This guy kind of freaks me out," Racer X explains. "When I meet him, he's always bobbing his head around and making it look like a drug deal." A few moments after we pull into the lot, Racer X calls the customer, a tall middle-aged man in a tank top and shorts who is actually waiting just a few yards away. He walks up, putting his cell phone away.

"I can give you two hundred bucks if you don't mind, or would you rather I give you what I owe you?" the man asks nervously.

"Your total is $140," Racer X says. "I can give you a fiver. Here you go."

The man laughs self-consciously as he puts the money in his wallet. He glances back and forth. "Ha, ha, ha," he says. "I'm getting used to this now."

We drive back to the Big Kahuna's house with $520 in cash in Racer X's briefcase. Today, he estimates that the Big Kahuna has made $1,000, and that, as a driver, he will receive $200. As we navigate the rush-hour traffic on Harbor Boulevard for the third or fourth time that evening, Racer X reflects on his volunteer work with the club. "This is a really cool job," he says. "The first few times I went out, I was really nervous. You don't know if you're going to be meeting a cop or a cowboy who might decide he wants the weed for free and pulls a gat on you. But that's never happened yet."

Racer X's closest call happened in a parking lot when he made the mistake of getting out of his car to hand an envelope to a customer in return for a wad of cash. An alert security guard saw the exchange and pulled up to ask what was going on. "I told him it was a medical-supply delivery," Racer X says. "He couldn't see what was in the envelopes and didn't really know what was going on, so he didn't call the cops."

Even if the guard had done so, Racer X says he's confident that he'd be protected. "Legally, we're fine," he says. "There is no problem with what we are doing. If a cop were to pull up in the middle of a delivery, I have a paper saying the patient has designated the club as his caregiver. I might run into a problem, but I would just keep my fucking mouth shut and not say a goddamn thing and see what happens in the courts."

That anecdote reminds Racer X of a funny story he'd been meaning to tell me all day. "Remember that cute girl we delivered to last week?" he asks, referring to Yoga Girl. "Well, her mom got hold of her cell phone." According to Racer X, Yoga Girl's mom began dialing all the unfamiliar numbers on her daughter's phone, which eventually put her on the line with the Big Kahuna, who always answers the phone by stating the name of his cannabis collective.

"What are you?" the anxious mother asked the Big Kahuna.

"We're a club," he offered.

"Is my daughter in your club?" the woman asked, the alarm in her voice rising.

The Big Kahuna was about to hang up the telephone, but then thought better of it. After all, it wasn't like he was a drug dealer.

Marijuana's legal now, he suddenly remembered, and he was the proud director of a legitimate nonprofit organization that happened to deliver medicine.

"Please answer my question," pleaded the woman on the other end of the line.

"Yeah, you know what?" the Big Kahuna responded, his voice still friendly and professional as he hung up on her. "I don't think I'm going to answer any more of your questions. You're not part of the club."

2 | The Big Kahuna's Club

The balloon is almost as tall as Racer X.

He unscrews it from the top of the Volcano-brand vaporizer, a stainless steel contraption that resembles the base of a blender. The vaporizer is perched on a bookshelf pushed up to one wall of the back room in the headquarters of the Big Kahuna's brand-new marijuana club. It has a dial set to well above 130 degrees, the temperature at which marijuana begins to release its medicinal THC into the atmosphere as a vapor.

It's just before 2:00 PM on this spring day in 2011, two years after my first ride-along with Racer X. He holds the balloon to his lips, his palms gently pressing at its sides. An invisible mist of vaporized marijuana forces its way deep into his lungs. He struggles to maintain his balance as he continues to inhale, his hands grasping the balloon much tighter now. He blows upward to the ceiling, coughing contentedly, then hands the balloon to his friend, who repeats the ritual.

On the couch behind Racer X are two knapsacks, both of which are partially unzipped. Clearly visible are a pair of large clear sacks that are bursting with marijuana that's already been divided into one-ounce quantities. The bags of marijuana have just been hand-delivered via courier from the Big Kahuna's nearby pot garden. By themselves, the two bags are worth thousands of dollars, but they represent just a tiny fraction of his harvest. The indoor grow house is at a secret location known only to the Big Kahuna and his partner, who's been providing the Big Kahuna with marijuana for about four years, ever since he was just a regular weed dealer. Now the two men have gone quasi-legitimate.

Their theater of operations is Costa Mesa, a sleepy Southern California city with just over one hundred thousand residents, a large number of whom are retired. It's sandwiched between Orange County's two socioeconomic extremes. To its south, on the coast, is the Republican yachting enclave of Newport Beach; to the north lies the working-class barrios of the county seat, Santa Ana, the majority of whose population is Latino and which has the highest percentage of foreign-born Mexicans in the country. Coast Mesa's biggest source of income is tax revenue from half of a high-end shopping mall, South Coast Plaza—the other half is owned by Santa Ana. Costa Mesa's city council is a generally conservative bunch, although the mayor, Gary Monahan, owns a bar and is rumored to be friendly, in a libertarian sort of way, to the notion of medical marijuana. For now, at least, pot clubs are being tolerated by the city so long as neighbors don't complain, and providing they promise to grow their own medicine rather than buy it on the underground market. Thus, the Big Kahuna simply arranged an exclusive arrangement with his friend, the latest fruits of which are in the knapsacks, ready for Racer X and his buddy to break open and divvy into plastic containers for delivery or purchase at the dispensary.

Dividing medical marijuana into ounce, half-ounce, quarter-ounce, and eighth-ounce amounts is just one of Racer X's new responsibilities. He also spends at least two mornings each week trimming recently harvested marijuana plants of their outer leaves, which are then processed into highly potent powder, or *kief*, as well as hashish, tinctures, and edible marijuana products. Savvy cannabis club operators like the Big Kahuna know they can more than double their revenues if they know how to properly trim their product.

Two years earlier, the club operated out of the Big Kahuna's rented, two-bedroom house. Now, he owns his own place, and with a wife, a toddler, and an infant son living with him, he no longer works from home. Back then, the Big Kahuna answered most of the incoming delivery calls himself, and he had only a few hundred customers who were served by Racer X and two other part-time drivers. Now, in the back room of the Big Kahuna's headquarters, a fleet of operators lined up at telephones along one wall answer a steady stream of delivery requests.

"Are you more of an indica guy?" one of the operators asks. "Well, this one is great for pain, but it'll knock you out, so be ready, boss."

There's also a storefront dispensary that's open from noon to 8:00 PM seven days a week. The Big Kahuna estimates that he has roughly twenty-five hundred members and that more than one hundred people walk through the doors of his dispensary each day. Despite the convenience, door-to-door deliveries now account for only 20 percent of his business, which he estimates grosses at least $75,000 per month. His is just one of roughly thirty dispensaries that have opened in this city in the past year, at the rate of one or two a month, with some dispensaries shuttering within a few months because of the stiff competition.

Racer X's main job is managing the storefront, which has a hip, tiki-style façade and looks at first blush like it might be a surfboard shop. There, he sits behind a desk and verifies incoming club members by checking to see that they are carrying a valid doctor's recommendation to smoke marijuana. He flirts with an attractive middle-aged blonde who's waiting for her verification. Racer X loves his new job much more than driving around in traffic, trying to find customers with a half-functioning GPS device. As soon as the storefront opened, in fact, he quit his day job at the grocery and began working the front office of Big Kahuna's dispensary. "He's working with customers full-time in the storefront, right where he belongs," the Big Kahuna explains. "It's a better place for him than out driving around doing deliveries. He's a people person, if you know what I mean."

Racer X is just one of thirty employees who work for the Big Kahuna, who recently obtained health insurance for his entire workforce. "Seventy-five thousand dollars in revenue sounds like a lot of cash," he says. "But I've got so much overhead. Plus, we're getting fined by the city's code-enforcement people at least twice a month, so that's another five thousand dollars off the top. Then there's advertising, legal fees, and lobbying expenses."

Still, the Big Kahuna has so much money leftover at the end of the month that he has to start giving the weed away. That's because, unlike Colorado, for example, which allows dispensaries to profit from sales, California state law requires cannabis clubs to operate as nonprofit corporations. Thus, frequent cannabis consumers in California know that the best time to purchase weed from a dispensary tends to be at the end of the month. "That's when we have to offer all these deals," the Big Kahuna says, "like buy one, get one free."

It being the end of the month, another phone rings and another operator picks up, answering in a cheerful voice by stating the name of the cannabis club. A few seconds later, another phone rings. Because the second operator is already on a call, a third employee takes picks up the receiver. "Can you hold, please?" he asks, before pushing a button to answer, yes, another call. "Yes, we deliver. One hour—tops—once you're verified. Can you hold, please?"

— — — — —

The headquarters of Big Kahuna's marijuana club is a white barn that he converted into a front lobby, rear living room, and loft. The building is located less than half a block from a freeway entrance, thus saving time for the delivery drivers in terms of swift commuter access. The proximity to a busy rush of traffic also offers the vaguely neurotic reassurance of escape should the feds or local cops choose to mount a raid. There's no sign out front bearing the collective's name, no green-cross logo painted on the wall hinting at what's inside.

Despite the low profile he maintains, rather than run from the cops, the Big Kahuna insists, he and other medical-marijuana dispensary owners want to work with them to follow state law. In 2010, along with half a dozen other cannabis club operators in coastal Orange County, the Big Kahuna formed a professional organization called the Orange County Director's Alliance, or OCDA for short. The acronym OCDA is something of a joke: it also stands for Orange County District Attorney, a distinctly non-pot-friendly entity. There's nothing funny about what the pro-marijuana OCDA is doing, however: just a few months into its existence, it pooled its resources to fund its very own candidate for the Costa Mesa city council. The candidate in question, Sue Lester, owner of Herban Elements, a marijuana dispensary, happens to be a dues-paying member of OCDA.

Unlike most dispensary owners, who tend to be young or middle-aged white males, Lester turned out to be a cheerful, petite brunette. I interviewed her at her shop in September 2010. Getting inside wasn't easy. First of all, I had to show my valid California driver's license and my doctor's note allowing me to smoke cannabis. This particular piece of paperwork I had obtained from a doctor conveniently located across the street from the *OC Weekly* office in Costa Mesa. My medical evaluation consisted of me filling out a two-page form on which I listed my symptoms—anxiety, insomnia, occasional back and neck pain—having my pulse taken, and paying one hundred dollars.

Once I showed Lester my paperwork and she was able to verify my doctor's note on her computer by clicking on the doctor's website and accessing my file with a password, she buzzed me through a locked door into the dispensary's small lobby. At this point, she was still secured behind yet another cashier's window accessible from the lobby side of the locked door. Beneath this window was a small collection of clipboards, each containing a lengthy questionnaire, the last page of which is a form that all first-time visitors must complete that established me as a brand-new member of Herban Elements' cannabis club. I filled it out while relaxing in one of two comfy chairs that were positioned in view of a flat-screen TV which was tuned to a classic-rock music station; Led Zeppelin's "Kashmir" played softly.

It all seemed very official, pretty much like visiting a new doctor for the first time and having to fill out all those annoying insurance forms, except I didn't also have to wait an hour. Once I'd successfully joined her collective, Lester buzzed me through a second door, behind which was a handsomely appointed, coffee shop–style bar crafted from wood. Shelves beneath the bar were stocked with knee braces, vitamins, herbal supplements, antiviral sprays, and other homeopathic health products. A refrigerator in the corner displayed various cannabis-laced baked goods—everything from peanut butter and jelly sandwiches to muffins, brownies, and cinnamon-streusel coffee cake. Stretching along the bar were gallon-sized jars full of every imaginable strain of cannabis.

More expensive strains—priced higher not because of superior quality but because they take longer to grow, Lester was careful to point out—were on view in a large cabinet. An antique gasoline pump stood in one corner near a couple of framed marijuana-themed posters, one of which asked, "GOD MADE GRASS, MAN MADE

BOOZE: WHO DO YOU TRUST?" A message on the chalkboard behind the bar asked all visitors to register to vote and, if they were a resident of Costa Mesa, to pull the lever for Lester in the November 2010 city council race.

Other than a few candidates in the Bay Area, Lester is the first marijuana-dispensary operator in American history to run for public office, something that put her in the unique position of being possibly able to run a city government that has been bent on putting her out of business. "I never thought I'd be running for public office," Lester told me. "But I don't agree with a lot of the things the city is doing or the methods they are using. I can sit here and do nothing and hope somebody else changes things, or I can raise my hand and do what I can for what I think is right."

About an hour into my interview with Lester, a string of patients began entering Herban Elements. She smilingly greeted each customer by name. Unlike some Southern California dispensaries that see up to two hundred patients per day, Lester told me her club averaged about twenty-five daily visits and has no more than one thousand members. "Our system is programmed to lock out new members when we reach maximum capacity," she explained. A year after forming as a nonprofit, Herban Elements still operated at a deficit, she said, because member donations were both paying for operating expenses and repaying the initial loan she used to finance the brick-and-mortar facility. The club also made monthly charitable donations with any leftover revenue; recipients included the American Cancer Society, Costa Mesa Senior Center, Costa Mesa Foundation for Parks and Recreation, AIDS Foundation OC, the Arthritis Foundation, and Orange Coast College's culinary program. Unlike most other cannabis collectives, there was no menu on the club's website. "There is no reason for anyone to see that kind of thing on the Internet," she explained. "Some kid can read about what you have and what you do, and we're not trying to incite people who have no business being there to have information about our establishment."

The first patient of the day was an elderly man with a plug in his throat connected to a breathing tube.

"Would you like some water?" Lester asked.

The man has to touch the plug on his throat to speak. "I'd love some," came the raspy reply. He took a sniff of one of Herban Elements' most popular pure indica strains, Stinky Pink, which was available for sixteen dollars per gram. (All of the cannabis at Herban Elements was priced from twelve to sixteen dollars per gram, or thirty-five to sixty dollars per eighth.)

Next through the door were two young men. One of them, a tall, lanky guy with close-cropped hair and mirrored aviator sunglasses, said he used to find his marijuana at the now-shuttered Doc's, which the city had raided a few months earlier. "It was a shit hole," he declared. "Here, they know my name. They give me free water. They know customer service."

His friend had a soul patch on his chin, several tattoos on his arm, and a wary expression on his face. "I came all the way from Anaheim," he announced, explaining he's recently been discharged from the military and is now attending college classes in Costa Mesa. "The main reason I come here," he added, "is they honor vets."

It's possible Lester's insistence on giving discounts to military veterans stems from her personal background. She's a registered Republican who grew up in a military family—her father served in the US Army in Korea shortly after the end of that war, and she boasts family members in "every branch of the service." She also has a long history of administrative jobs in the private sector, mostly in human resources and employee relations, for a variety of retail and manufacturing companies she prefers not to mention by name.

After growing up and graduating from Ganesha High School in Pomona, just across the L.A. County line from Brea, where she was born in 1967, Lester took classes in administration of justice at Mount San Antonio College in Walnut, California, aiming to be a police officer. Because she planned to raise a family, however, Lester dropped the idea and ended up working for the next decade at the "national retailer best known for customer service" in a security-related capacity that required her to "reduce shrinkage" by making sure "everybody followed the rules and nobody took anything home with them they weren't supposed to have."

In 1999, after spending two years in Texas helping the retailer open southwestern regional outlets, she moved to Orange County and spent the next two years completing a culinary program at Orange Coast College while also working full-time as a pastry chef. From 2003 to 2008, Lester went back into corporate management, this time for a Compton-based manufacturing company for which she created a human-resources department that oversaw the company's expansion into China, as well as a workforce that swelled from twenty-two to more than five hundred employees. She lasted five years, until a series of illnesses and family deaths put her on a new path in life.

In 2008, her father, who had already been diagnosed with prostate cancer, suffered a heart attack, and underwent heart bypass surgery. Her mom went to the hospital for knee and back operations, the latter to repair a degenerative spine condition that had caused severe pain. In the midst of all that, Lester's grandmother, a great-uncle, an aunt, and a cousin all died from long-term illnesses. Shortly before her grandmother died in January 2009, a friend of Lester's suggested she offer her ailing relative an edible marijuana brownie. The doctor green-lit the proposal, so Lester—who had recently obtained her own doctor's note to use medical marijuana to treat arthritis and joint pain, the latter caused by old sports injuries—brought a brownie to the hospital room. "She took a bite and spit it out," Lester recalled. "I tasted it, and it tasted horrible, like dirt and plant matter with this sweet chocolate slathered on top of it."

Because of Lester's experience as a chef, she "started toying around with the idea that I can make things that taste better," she says. A state-certified chef, Lester personally bakes all the edibles sold at Herban Elements and at a nearby restaurant run by a friend of hers.

Just a few weeks after her grandmother passed away, Lester began researching Senate Bill 420, which regulates cannabis clubs. "The more I read, the more I realized that not everybody was operating within the law," she said. "The first place I went to was in Hollywood, and it was in a really scary part of town where I had to park four blocks away and walk past prostitutes and pimps and crackheads to get there. They weren't asking for the right information from patients or verifying them, and there were places where people were medicating on-site, and it happened to have a lot of things besides cannabis, like cocaine. I realized not all these places were in accordance with the spirit of medical marijuana, which is about helping people with serious medical problems, as opposed to being in furtherance of somebody's party."

In mid-2009, Lester drove to Costa Mesa City Hall, walked upstairs to the planning department, and applied for a city business license to sell natural remedies, health supplies, and herbal supplements. She knew full well that, four years earlier, the city had drafted an ordinance prohibiting medical-marijuana dispensaries from operating there. "I didn't write 'medical marijuana' out on my application because I was told by a number of people—attorneys, people who work for cities—that cities don't want a gigantic influx of these types of businesses, which I understand," Lester said. "I wrote 'herbal supplements, vitamins, and joint supports,' which is all stuff we have here. So if you call the city and ask them if they've issued any permits or business licenses for medical marijuana, they can say no, because they haven't. They told me that by doing that, you are helping the city as well as helping yourself."

At the time, only two other dispensaries operated in Costa Mesa: One of them was MedMar, which now shares the same office building as Herban Elements. The other was Doc's, which was located on Newport Boulevard at the end of the Costa Mesa Freeway. But in the few months between obtaining her license and renovating the space that would become Herban Elements, more than a dozen other collectives had sprouted up throughout Costa Mesa. According to the city, none of these businesses is operating legally. Claire Flynn, a principal planner with Costa Mesa, told me, "We have not allowed business licenses to be approved for any business that represents itself as a medical-marijuana dispensary. It's considered a prohibited use." The sudden influx led to a rapid deterioration of relations between cannabis clubs and city government and thrust Lester into her historic bid for public office.

The first time the cops came to Herban Elements was on March 4, 2010, exactly a month after police carried out their first major dispensary raid of the year against West Coast Wellness, arresting three men for suspicion of marijuana sales. Lester knew about the raid but wasn't worried about her club because she felt confident she was operating well within state law. Lester was in her car, about to run an errand, when several police cruisers and city code–enforcement vehicles pulled into the parking lot. "I was in the driveway," she recalled. "I drove around the block and came back, and they were all standing in the parking lot. I walked up and said good morning to everybody and went back upstairs." She saw the cops knock on the door of MedMar, the other collective in her building. Then they knocked on her door. "They said they were here to issue me a cease-and-desist order," she recalled. "I asked why, and they said I was operating without a valid business license."

When Lester pointed at the business license on her wall, the officers accused her of lying on her application form by not specifying she would be providing medical marijuana. "I told them I wasn't a criminal and that other than an occasional parking ticket, I've never broken any law. They said if they came back and I was still operating, they would cite me."

Lieutenant Mark Manley, a spokesman for the Costa Mesa Police Department, told me that officers heard through code enforcement that a number of medical-marijuana dispensaries were attempting to open in the city. "As we looked into it, information came to our attention that at some dispensaries there were criminal sales of marijuana going on above and beyond the intent of the Compassionate Use Act." Manley said. "Through investigation, we were able to discern that was the case, and we did criminal filings on both of them."

Manley added that raids have only been carried out against West Coast Wellness and Doc's to date, but investigations against other collectives continue. He drew a distinction between criminal probes and code-enforcement actions the police helped carry out against dispensaries such as Herban Elements that are simply suspected of operating outside the city's municipal code. "It's not an issue of whether medical marijuana is right or not, but whether these operations are allowed to exist in Costa Mesa, and none of them are," he said. "We'll see what happens in November," he added. "The climate is changing, and the police department will change with it. Whatever comes down from the voters and city hall, we'll follow. There's this belief that the police department is philosophically against medical marijuana, but that's not true."

Lester ran a business-friendly political campaign that focused on raising revenue for Costa Mesa's cash-strapped coffers. She attended city council meetings and spoke about the need for the city to cooperate with businesses like hers that are providing jobs to local residents as well as providing them with a service that is protected under state law. She also met with crew-cut representatives of the police officers' union, who listened as she glowingly recalled her upbringing in a military family and how she got into the medical cannabis industry because of sick relatives whose doctors suggested they try marijuana, and—perhaps most relevant, boys—how she just wants to preserve important city services such as the police.

Lester already knew some of the cops firsthand. They'd shown up at her collective a few times asking questions and warning her that if she didn't shut down, she'd be hit with major fines and could be subject to a raid herself. But after hearing her story, and upon realizing that if elected to the council, Lester could be a strong ally in their efforts to save their own jobs by finding new revenue streams, several officers told her they'd proudly place her campaign signs in their front yards. In the end, however, the change in momentum came too late and Lester came second to last in a field of five candidates for the open council seat. Costa Mesa wasn't ready for a cannabis candidate, after all.

– – – – –

Max Del Real is a suit-wearing, square-jawed man who looks like an actor who plays a politician on prime-time television and spends his free time pumping iron in the gym. He's sitting on a couch opposite his client, the Big Kahuna. An hour earlier, Del Real, whose idea it was to have Lester run for city council, arrived from Sacramento at Orange County's John Wayne Airport. Today, he's in town to make a public, televised presentation to the city council later this evening about the advantages of working with his clients to create a medical-marijuana ordinance that serves the city's needs.

Del Real has done all this before—in his hometown, Sacramento. In 2009, the state capital experienced an onslaught of medical-marijuana clubs. The city had no regulations in place to dictate how it should respond. The same thing had just happened in San Francisco, which tolerated the explosion of dispensaries, and Oakland, which shuttered forty-five clubs simultaneously before announcing that only four clubs would receive a permit, and would have to competitively apply.

"Sacramento did not want to be another San Francisco, but they didn't want to be another Oakland, either," Del Real tells me. "So they sent registration letters to the thirty-nine clubs in the city and invite them to apply for permits, with a total of twelve permits to be awarded." Fifteen of those dispensaries reacted by forming a group called the Sacramento Alliance, collecting dues, holding votes, and meeting at a local restaurant. It was at one of those meetings that one of the dispensary owners, who happened to know Del Real from high school, urged his colleagues to hire him to lobby Sacramento's city council. At the next meeting, Del Real showed up and introduced himself and his plan.

"I'm gonna lobby the decision makers," he told the worried gathering of pot purveyors. "I'm going to start with the mayor. I'm going to work the council, the city manager's office, reach out to economic development, talk to planning and police, because I believe in Jesus Christ my savior, guns, and baseball, in that order, and tell them we're here to work with you, not against you."

An hour after he left the meeting, Del Real got the call that he'd been hired. He immediately began lobbying Sacramento's political leadership. His first telephone call went to the person Del Real describes as the "biggest asshole" on the city council, vice mayor Robbie Waters, a former sheriff's deputy who "killed two people on the job and got away with it, because you can do that when you're a cop," and a conservative Republican who openly berated medical marijuana as a criminal scam devised by dopers who belonged behind bars.

"Mr. Waters," Del Real said, "I'd like to buy you a drink."

"Sounds good to me," Waters replied.

"And talk about medical cannabis," Del Real quickly added.

A few days later, over beers, Del Real pitched his clients to Waters. "I'll be honest with you," he said. "This is not about medicine. This is about jobs. This is about public safety and revenue for the city of Sacramento. We're pro-business. I know you're a big flag-waving American and so are my people. You'd be surprised that half of them are Republicans like you, Robbie. This isn't about pot, this is about politics, and we are trying to work with you here."

Next, Del Real reached out to the rest of the city council, inviting them all to meet his clients at luncheons set up away from the dispensaries. "We got face time with the decision makers," he says. "They saw that they were making a decision about thirty-nine businesses, many of which have ten to twenty full-time employees supporting families, saving for college. I made my first phone call in March 2009, and in June the council voted to extend its moratorium on new clubs, but not to shut down any of the thirty-nine clubs that were already there." The city then passed a medical cannabis ordinance that grandfathered in Del Real's clients. "We celebrated that night, I can tell you," he recalls. "I can't tell you how we celebrated because that's client privilege, but it was a big moment for medical marijuana in California."

That victory explains why for the past several months the Big Kahuna, who just two years earlier was delivering weed out of his rented house, has been paying Del Real to fly down to Costa Mesa and lobby that city's elected leadership to pass a similar ordinance. Del Real is certain that day will soon come. "Costa Mesa should do exactly what Sacramento did and pass a zoning ordinance with a variance for grandfather rights," he said. "I've told this to the mayor, and I will again when I meet with him tomorrow: Costa Mesa could emerge as a model city, effectively regulating medical cannabis for all of Southern California. And I think that's very exciting."

What's even more exciting, Del Real tells me, is that one day soon, qualified patients from any US state where medical marijuana is legal will be able to travel to California to obtain medicine. This is already the law in Montana, where medical marijuana patients can travel outside the state to obtain medicine from marijuana dispensaries elsewhere. Nevada's medical marijuana law, on the other hand, only allows patients to grow their own plants, not to purchase cannabis at a dispensary. "There is not one permitted dispensary in the Silver State, not one," Del Real says. "You cannot get medical cannabis in Nevada unless you grow it yourself, in your closet."

Such restrictions don't bother Del Real in the least. In fact, he argues, it's a business opportunity for California. "It's called reciprocity," he explains, "and it's the next phase on the road to legalization. There are state politicians I'm talking to right now that fully accept and are starting to examine the idea of reciprocity of patient basis. If we import patients, California will be able to export medicine, and that's a fact. It's a brave new world."

— — — — —

The attorney's BlackBerry won't stop buzzing.

Locked on vibrate, it skids along the surface of the cafeteria-style table before a bald, bespectacled man in a tweed suit and vest, white pressed shirt, and paisley tie who is eating an undressed salad. Although he's a Harley-riding triathlete and an amateur mixed-martial artist whose claim to fame is tapping out champion Joe Rogan, Christopher Glew bears an uncanny resemblance to the comedian David Cross of *Arrested Development* fame. Having just raced back to work in his late-model Mercedes SUV from a morning at the Orange County Superior Courthouse, Glew is eating a late lunch inside the ground-floor cafeteria of the Xerox building in Santa Ana, eight floors beneath the law office where he has built a successful practice representing medical-marijuana collectives throughout California, including the Big Kahuna's.

Unable to ignore the buzzing phone any longer, Glew finally takes the call; his eyebrows furrow as he listens to another of his clients, calling to say he's about to be arrested.

"Just don't say anything," Glew instructs in a calm, matter-of-fact tone of voice. "No matter what, don't answer any questions. If they've already raided you, that means they've already made up their mind that what you're doing is illegal, so there's no point in talking."

As soon as Glew hangs up, his phone rings again, this time from another client in Northern California whose club is being simultaneously raided. "If you're not there, don't go there," he says. "Stay where you are."

Moments later, a third call comes in. "My advice would be to turn yourself in," he suggests.

Once off the phone, Glew shakes his head. "I would never endorse a club that wasn't willing to sit down with the DA to work something out," he tells me. "But the problem is, the DA will always tell you what you're doing wrong, but they'll never say what you're doing right. Everyone thinks what they are doing is legal, so why shouldn't they talk? But in the fifty cases I've done, every single thing the clubs did to become legitimate was used against them."

Of course, Glew is well aware that the true industry leaders in the medical-marijuana business operate in a different world than his clients, the dispensary owners and operators who are at constant risk of being raided. These players, he says, belong to statewide networks that bridge the gap between Northern and Southern California. "People make a big deal about the 'disconnect' between Northern and Southern California, when in reality they're completely intertwined and there really is no disconnect," Glew argues. "The people that are really controlling the future of this industry, if they are relevant, they have a presence in Northern and Southern California. You'd have to talk to someone in the know, but the ideal circumstances for a large-scale marijuana producer would be to be able to control all your growing conditions."

Indoor growing, in other words, is far more efficient and profitable than growing outdoors, where you have to depend on Mother Nature. That's why, fifteen years ago, 90 percent of California's marijuana was cultivated in what law enforcement calls "the Emerald Triangle," the three Northern California counties of Humboldt, Trinity, and Mendocino, whereas today, Southern California produces as much, if not more, high-end marijuana as the Triangle. "As laws have liberalized and people have become more entrepreneurial and medical marijuana has expanded its reach throughout the state, by the simple machinations of industry, it's become easier to not have to transport significant quantities," Glew adds. "That's still the number-one problem."

Transportation.

Without it, the marijuana that comes out of the ground in Mendocino or Ferndale stays in the ground, and the high-tech indoor strains being cooked up by whiz-kid botanists fresh out of Cal Berkeley remain locked inside warehouses in Oakland and Los Angeles. No transportation? The shelves of countless dispensaries stay empty. No transportation, no marijuana industry. For distributors like the Big Kahuna and erstwhile deliverymen like Racer X, the risks aren't just low, they're essentially zero—nothing more than a few uncomfortable minutes showing paperwork to a police officer before you're on your way.

But for the weed runners, and it is they who truly keep the weed industry running, the stakes are astronomically high. With one hundred or two hundred pounds of freshly harvested marijuana in your trunk, the difference between making a quick fortune and spending the rest of your life in jail can amount to something as trivial as a broken taillight or a faulty speedometer. That kind of weight, any more than, say, twenty pounds, depending on how good your lawyer is and how well you know the law, wins you automatic jail time.

"If you're doing an eight-hour, ten-hour road trip, there are a lot of issues that can come up between locations," Glew tells me, and it's clear the speed traps and checkpoints of the Emerald Triangle have yielded him a crop of clients. "I mean, you're either going to have the cash or you're going to have the product, and either way, you're going to have some explaining to do."

3 | Low-Hanging Fruit

The driver of the white Honda Civic was in a rush.

Traffic was light in the northbound lane of Highway 101, so California Highway Patrol officers J. A. Slates and C. Cotroneo had no trouble spotting the speeding vehicle. In the southbound lane, Slates slammed on the brakes, swerved through the grassy median, and pulled a screeching U-turn, burning rubber in pursuit of the offender. Cotroneo switched on the radar, clocked the Honda hauling ass at eighty mph, turned on the lights, and hit the sirens.

At 8:58 PM on June 28, 2009, near the Mendocino County town of Ukiah, the Honda pulled over to the side of the freeway and rolled to a stop. As Slates approached the car, he noticed the driver "making furtive movements," according to his police report. He walked up to the passenger-side window, and the driver then rolled it down to surrender his driver's license, at which point, Slates would later claim, he smelled a strong odor of marijuana.

Slates escorted the driver to the patrol car and searched the Honda, quickly finding "several marijuana joints in the ashtray, a burnt joint in the front passenger seat, two green containers of marijuana next to the ashtray, a white bag containing four green containers of marijuana, four smaller clear containers of hashish, three marijuana pipes with residue, miscellaneous marijuana paraphernalia, and an unused pipe."

The driver, Mark Gregory Moen, claimed he was tired because he'd been driving for ten to eleven hours. He freely admitted he had smoked pot a few hours earlier, and handed the officers a prescription that allowed him to smoke medical marijuana under California's Compassionate Use Act. Moen volunteered to take a field sobriety test, which he passed. But when the two officers ran Moen's license through their laptop computer, they discovered he was wanted in connection with a three-year-old burglary in Southern California. After placing him under arrest, the officers prepared to have his car towed into town. That's when Moen told Slates he needed something from the trunk: $72,000 in cash.

Slates confiscated the money and put in an alert to the Mendocino County Major Crimes Task Force. He suspected Moen was likely rushing to Humboldt County to purchase marijuana and knew there was a good chance the task force could confiscate the cash. What Slates didn't know: he'd just busted the owner of the one of the biggest medical-marijuana dispensaries south of San Francisco.

— — — — —

From the looks of it, Orange County Men's Jail inmate No. 2561040 has had a pretty tough weekend. Deep grooves in his forehead and concentric circles of worry lines that surround his eyes suggest he hasn't been sleeping particularly well. Moen's skin is sallow; his tousled, matted, dark hair is speckled with white and gray; and his teeth are looking a bit yellow. Moen, fifty, is hunched over in evident discomfort behind a thick glass window, squirming on a small metal stool. He's struggling to hold onto a telephone, which isn't easy because both of his hands are restrained in handcuffs that are attached to a chain around his waist.

I'm visiting Moen this spring afternoon because he never returned my telephone call. A few weeks earlier, when I first spoke to him, he'd told me about his bimonthly runs to Humboldt County, explaining that he had old friends there who grew marijuana and that this is where he obtained the medicine for his cannabis club, which was located in a Lake Forest mini-mall next door to a Montessori preschool—and two doors down from yet another dispensary, Vale Tudo Café. I figured Moen would make an interesting travel companion to the Emerald Triangle, someone who could help me capture the intensity of driving in and out of America's marijuana heartland with a trunk full of cash or contraband. Unfortunately, it appears, the cops caught up with him before I could.

"I'm on the chain list," Moen explains apologetically, after the phone slips off his right shoulder a few sentences into our conversation at the jail. The chains are a security precaution courtesy of his past criminal record, which included several stints in prison for burglary that led to an unfortunate habit of fighting in jail. "That happened a long time ago," Moen says, wincing with embarrassment. "It wasn't easy being the only white guy in jail, you know, but that's no excuse. That's not who I am now, though. I'm a different person, but they won't even let me brush my teeth. I haven't had a comb or a toothbrush in four days!"

Moen has been behind bars since March 5, 2010, the day several sheriff's deputies raided 215 Agenda, Moen's now-defunct marijuana dispensary in Lake Forest, for the second time in several months. Prosecutors charged him with thirty-eight felony counts of money laundering, one felony count of possession of money amounting to more than $100,000 obtained from illegal sales of marijuana, three felony counts of selling marijuana, and one count of possessing marijuana with the intent to sell.

Before the Lake Forest raid, Moen had agreed to let me tag along with him on his next run through the Emerald Triangle. Moen had already been busted in Ukiah. I'd asked Moen when he thought he'd be heading north again. "I'm going up this Friday," he'd told me. "I have to appear in court that day in Ukiah." I'd tried to explain to Moen that I wasn't talking about his next court date, but his next weed run through the Emerald Triangle. "Like I said, I've got to be in Ukiah on Friday," he'd responded, as if unaware just how crazy and risky that sounded.

The Ukiah bust was a harbinger of a series of unfortunate incidents for Moen and 215 Agenda that culminated with a raid on his house. The next one happened about 11:45 PM on September 30, 2009, as Moen drove through Huntington Beach, a town known throughout Southern California for its overzealous law enforcement officers, who are particularly fond of arresting drunk drivers. The town likes to call itself Surf City, and is infamous for its rowdy Main Street, which is lined on both sides by dive bars and loud, obnoxious nightclubs with names such as Hurricanes Bar & Grill that are frequented by strippers, porn stars, and heavily tattooed bodybuilders. Anybody stupid enough to drink and drive late at night in this town can fully expect to get busted.

Moen was fiddling with the global-positioning device on his dashboard when a Surf City cop pulled him over for swerving on the road. Just as in Ukiah, the officer smelled pot and searched the car. Although he allowed Moen to drive away after examining paperwork showing that Moen owned a pot dispensary, he searched the vehicle first and confiscated another $145,000 in cash, which Moen claimed was the proceeds of roughly eight days of business. In the ever-changing world of criminal penalties for marijuana, the maximum amount of marijuana any one person is allowed to possess has fluctuated wildly. Two years ago, the allowed amount was twelve immature or six flowering plants at home and up to eight ounces locked up in your truck. Nowadays, if you have a good lawyer, the maximum amount you can carry is whatever the court agrees is "reasonable."

One thing that hasn't changed is the fact that if the cops catch you with, say, twenty or one hundred pounds of pot or tens or hundreds of thousands of dollars in cash, they're going to arrest you on drug trafficking charges, medical-marijuana card or not.

So in retrospect, it's no surprise that shortly after Moen was pulled over by Huntington Beach's finest, and as word spread of the cash haul, the Orange County Sheriff's Department, which patrols the Lake Forest neighborhood where 215 Agenda was located, began investigating the dispensary. At its peak, by Moen's own estimation, 215 Agenda served some two hundred customers per day. For the next month, sheriff's investigators monitored the dispensary and sent at least one undercover deputy carrying a doctor's note into the club to buy pot. On November 13, 2009, sheriff's deputies raided 215 Agenda and another Lake Forest dispensary, the Health Collective; confiscated financial records and patient information; and arrested both Moen, who bailed out of jail the next morning, and the Health Collective's owner, Steven Wick.

On March 5, deputies raided 215 Agenda again, this time arresting Moen and two store managers, Robert Adam Moody and Marco Enrique Verduzco, both twenty-three-years-old. The sheriff's search warrant from the second raid noted that 215 Agenda had placed advertisements in *OC Weekly* for "free marijuana" for first-time customers who mentioned the ad, which boasted, WE CARRY THE BEST WEED IN THE ENTIRE WORLD!

Moen is the first person to admit that selling marijuana—and selling it cheap—is exactly what 215 Agenda was all about. "I had no idea 215 Agenda would get so big," he says. "But nobody had ever heard of fifty dollar eighths, and that's what we offered. There's a reason we had five thousand patients. Wouldn't you want to get your weed as cheaply as possible?" He is also quick to acknowledge that his lengthy rap sheet doesn't exactly make him the ideal poster boy for medical marijuana.

If convicted, thanks to various sentencing enhancements, including one stemming from the 2006 burglary case, Moen could spend the next four decades behind bars. Of course, that's assuming he's crazy enough to actually fight this case in court rather than enter a guilty plea in return for a reduced sentence. Yet Moen appears to be exactly that crazy. "I didn't do anything wrong," he insists. "It would be a lie if I said I was guilty. I'm not taking any deal."

Shortly before I visited Moen at the jail, Christopher Glew had stopped by to talk to him. Although Glew wasn't representing Moen in his criminal case, Moen and several other Lake Forest dispensary owners had hired Glew to fight the city's civil lawsuit seeking to force them out of town. "I know Mark was trying to obey the law," Glew told me. "He says he was making monthly payments to the state board of equalization. If that's true, that shows he was trying to operate within the law. They are picking on Mark because he's an easy target. There are more raids going on now than when the feds were the only ones doing it. It's going to get worse before it gets better."

Earlier that morning, at the Orange County Superior Courthouse, Glew had sparred with a Lake Forest city attorney who was asking the judge to retroactively prohibit a dozen dispensaries from doing business there, including Moen's now-shuttered 215 Agenda. "We are here lawfully asserting our police power's right to defend the health and safety and public protection of the people of Lake Forest," Jeffrey Dunne, representing the city, had told Judge David R. Chaffee. "Marijuana is illegal under federal law."

Glew countered that because the city did not have an ordinance specifically outlawing cannabis clubs, it had no right to retroactively enforce such a ban. "Everything the collectives are doing is mandated by state law," he argued. "The city is just making up this category of marijuana dispensaries to make them look bad. They don't know what these clubs are because they are private. They're not open to the public."

I also spoke with Moen's court-appointed defense attorney, Derek Bercher. "Mark is a good person," Bercher told me. "He was trying to help people. He was trying to do a good thing in the right way, but he got caught up in the vagaries of the law." By "vagaries," Bercher is referring to the fact that prosecutors are claiming that every bank deposit or payroll transaction Moen made on behalf of 215 Agenda is evidence that he laundered cash from drug sales. "Mark couldn't have been more aboveboard," Bercher insisted. "For a supposed criminal, he was hiding in plain sight. Everything was through banks. He was donating to charities and libraries. The DA has a view that you simply cannot distribute medical marijuana without running afoul of the law."

The DA's press release on the raid served as a warning to anyone else contemplating a high-volume marijuana dispensary in Orange County. "Distribution and sale of marijuana to individuals with a physician's recommendation without any other relationship, such as through a dispensary, is not permitted under California law," it declared. "The three defendants are accused of selling marijuana to any person with a physician's recommendation without any relationship to the purchaser and without requiring or requesting them to participate in collectively or cooperatively growing marijuana."

Although some cannabis dispensaries try to stay on the good side of the law by insisting that all their marijuana is grown locally by club members—as opposed to being trucked south from Humboldt County, as in the case of 215 Agenda—Jeff Schunk, the deputy DA prosecuting Moen, believes that the law prohibits all dispensaries simply by virtue of the fact that they sell marijuana. "We believe what they are doing is illegal," he told me, asserting that only a "primary caregiver" can provide marijuana to a patient. "The wording of the state law is what it is, and it means you have to have consistently assumed responsibility for the housing, health, or safety of the patient."

Schunk's outlook neatly captures the insanity at the heart of medical marijuana law. Proposition 215, which created a framework for legal cultivation and possession of marijuana, was written so vaguely and inconsistently that police can bust anyone they choose for distributing the drug. Critics of prosecutors who continue to build medical marijuana cases claim that they're simply going after "low-hanging fruit," picking and choosing candidates for prosecution based on prior arrests and other character flaws, or by going after whatever dispensary seems to be handling the biggest volume of sales.

DA spokeswoman Susan Kang Schroeder claimed that all cases handled by her office are "fact-driven" and examined on an individual basis. "We are looking at the facts and circumstances of each case," she said. "It's a fantasy to suggest that these people are being wrongfully prosecuted." Schunk also insisted his office isn't out to get medical-marijuana smokers. "It is really well established that if you have a valid recommendation from a licensed doctor and all indications are you possess marijuana for medical uses, there's no reason for an arrest," he said.

– – – – –

Until he landed in jail, Moen had been living in the same one-story, three-bedroom house in Westminster in which he had grown up, the one that witnessed his chaotic evolution from 1970s punk rocker and surf bum to present-day medical-marijuana martyr. Moen grew up in Northern California but moved to Orange County during junior high school. Because he lived so close to the beach, he would often ditch classes, hop on a bus, and ride down Goldenwest Avenue to surf the bluffs north of the Huntington Beach pier.

He started using cocaine at age sixteen. "A lot of people in my high school had coke," he says. "I liked it and started injecting it." One time, a rich friend injected him with a mixture of coke and heroin. "He did that without telling me, but I liked it. You feel like God for a couple of seconds on coke, but then you feel really shitty. But with the heroin, you feel like you're in the eddy of a stormy sea."

When Moen turned eighteen in the late 1970s, his parents divorced and he moved in with his grandmother in Huntington Beach. He spent the next six years there, although he admits that most of the time, he wasn't sleeping at his grandmother's home, but rather in his Oldsmobile Delta 88, which he usually parked in Santa Monica. "I just surfed and skated," Moen recalls.

Before long, Moen's drug habit had led to several stints in jail. His parents disowned him, and he fell in with a group of surfers he describes as "basically a bunch of thieves who are now doing twenty-five-to-life." Their lifestyle consisted of surfing, shooting heroin, and stealing money from other surfers.

By far the most karmic (and bizarre) arrest in Moen's long history of burglaries was the time he was arrested for shoplifting at a Home Depot. "I tried to walk out of the store with a Moen water faucet so I could resell it for drugs," he says, shaking his head at the absurdity. "Instead, I went to state prison."

Moen met his wife in March 1998, shortly after being released, and the two quickly fell in love. "On our first date, Mark came and picked me up, and then I pretty much ditched him," Jennifer recalls. "I was using drugs at the time, and I wanted to protect him from that because I knew he was trying not to do that because he had just gotten out." But it wasn't long before both were using heroin together and getting in more trouble. In August 1998, the pair was convicted of stealing a car. Jennifer spent 120 days in jail, and Mark went back to state prison for a three-year sentence.

In the next eight years, Moen managed to hold down a grueling job as a pipefitter for an oil refinery company, working more than eighty hours per week, and fathered three children: Justin, seven; Jacquelyn, three; and Jagger, one. Raising a family introduced some stability into his life, but only temporarily. Jennifer fell back into drug use after becoming addicted to painkillers following her first pregnancy. "From 2003 to 2006, things got pretty bad again," she says. "But we ended up getting sober again."

The burglary case that led to Moen's arrest in Ukiah happened during this dark period in his life. Moen remembers little more than waking up in an office building he'd broken into the night before, shortly after he got into an argument with his wife and left the house in a drug-fueled rage. He hadn't stolen anything that night, although he'd planned to, and apparently the police had finally traced him through DNA he unwittingly left at the crime scene.

That same year, Moen fell ill with hepatitis C and had to submit to weekly chemotherapy treatments that left him nauseated and unable to eat. "I lost sixty-five pounds, and my hair was falling out," Moen says. His gastrointestinal doctor recommended he smoke marijuana to ease the nausea and increase his appetite. "I had to drive up to L.A., and OG Kush was selling for ninety dollars an eighth, which I couldn't afford."

His frustration with the high prices and long distances faced by patients in Orange County inspired him to form a collective closer to home. After spending months doing research at the Orange County law library and contacting various city agencies to inquire about applying for permits, Moen learned that the only city in the county where he could operate a cannabis club without a business license was Lake Forest. On April 20, 2009, Moen opened 215 Agenda in a somewhat dilapidated storefront in a nondescript mini-mall off El Toro Road near Interstate 5.

Two factors helped ensure the club would be a success. First was the fact that 215 Agenda offered premium-quality cannabis for fifty dollars an eighth instead of the seventy-five dollars or more charged by most dispensaries in Orange County; the club also audaciously advertised in the *OC Weekly* that first-time customers would receive a free "pre-roll" or joint or an edible marijuana product for joining up. Another factor was the dispensary's proximity to the retirement community Leisure World, which quickly formed a solid customer base for Moen's operation.

Before long, 215 Agenda was pulling in hundreds of thousands of dollars per month. "We had $50,000 per month going to Wells Fargo for payroll and $15,000 going to state taxes," Moen says. "We gave free marijuana to every new patient and to every returning patient." To meet his patients' rising demand for medical marijuana, Moen drove north to Humboldt County in Northern California every two weeks to meet with growers who were members of his collective, returning to Orange County with up to $100,000 worth of marijuana per trip.

Everything went smoothly until late June 2009. Moen, who usually made the bimonthly trip north with a few friends, was going alone for the first time, and Jennifer was worried because of that and it was a long drive. "I woke up at some point in the night—around three in the morning—and called him, and he didn't answer," she says. "And I kept calling and he didn't answer, so I knew something was wrong. Then he called me in the morning and said he'd been arrested for a warrant in Orange County."

On November 13, while deputies were raiding 215 Agenda, Jennifer was running errands. She called her husband at work just as sheriff's deputies raided the club and was told by him, "I'm getting robbed. There are people with ski masks coming through the door." She called 911, and an operator promised to get back to her with any news. The next call she got was from her neighbor, who told her there were cops all over her house.

"They kicked my door in and just wrecked our house," she says. "There wasn't any money at the house, but they pulled out some of Mark's plants and took all our computers and cameras." Although deputies didn't visit the house again until March 5, when they raided 215 Agenda the second time and arrested her husband, Jennifer says she constantly worries they will show up once more. "It's scary," she says. "It affects your security. It freaks you out."

She's not working and has three kids to take care of with little support from friends and family. Her older son has had trouble dealing with his dad's arrest. He says he hates cops and that he's tired of everyone telling him he has to take care of his mom. Although he's doing well in school, he acts out at home and refuses to do his homework. "He's just a kid," Jennifer says. "He needs to be a kid, but he also needs to do his homework. Sometimes I freak out on the kids because it's hard. Am I resentful? I cry every day. This has torn our family apart. I'm lost without Mark and don't know how to pick up the pieces."

— — — — —

Back inside the Orange County Jail's visiting area, on the other side of the thick, heavily scratched plastic window, Mark Moen has been talking for nearly two hours and is still going strong, despite the phone constantly slipping from his shoulder and the metal chain around his waist riding up his back.

"These things are biting into me," he complains, shifting his weight on the small stool. "The day I got arrested was my son, Justin's, first day of Little League," he says, tears welling up. "I used to play catch with him every day. If they give me thirty-nine years, I'll die in prison."

Of all the terrible things he's done in his life that Moen regrets, there's one that brings even more tears to his eyes. During the eight or so years Moen worked as a pipefitter, he says, he got to know a hardworking coworker. "This guy was a Christian, and I used to give him a hard time about it," Moen recalls. "He was such a nice guy, and I could be so mean. I insulted him, but he was always so happy. He worked so hard because he had six kids, and one day, he was driving home and was so tired he crashed his fucking car because he fell asleep driving home to see his family."

Moen grimaces at the memory. "He changed my life," he says, starting to sob now. "He made my life better. I spoke at his funeral, and that's what I said." Moen puts his two handcuffed palms in front of his face and rubs his eyes. "He made my life better. That's what he taught me. Pass the goodness on to other people. That's what I was trying to do, and that's how I want people to remember me."

For weed runners, the moral of Moen's story is simple: don't drive up and down Highway 101 with a car full of pot and cash and expect to get away with it for long. The vast majority of marijuana haulers—not to mention dispensary operators like Moen—never take such risks. Instead, they travel independently of the load, so that if the police intervene, they are nowhere near the merchandise. The closest they come to smuggling weed is flying the friendly skies with their personal stash in their carry-on luggage and a criminal defense attorney sitting by their side in case there are any problems.

4 | Prophets and Profiteers

A tiny American flag flaps in the breeze.

Its pole is stuck in the soil of a small potted plant. The patriotic display is part of the paltry yard décor bracketing the doorstep of the C3 Patients Association, which is located on the first floor of a gray office building on an access road in an industrial area of Garden Grove. Inside, behind the welcome desk manned by two young employees and the vault—a locked, antiseptic, humidor-type room with shelves of cannabis indica, sativa, and hybrids—there's a hallway with a display case full of glass pipes and other smoking paraphernalia. Beyond that is an office, where, seated behind a small desk, is a six-foot-seven man with a baby face and a booming voice.

With his short-sleeve polo shirt tucked into a pair of factory-washed jeans, Steele Smith bears no resemblance to the stereotypical red-eyed, tie-dyed, longhaired marijuana grower; he looks much more like a cop or a car salesman. But as the owner and operator of Orange County's second-oldest medical-marijuana collective, Smith has seen more than his fair share of such types as well as even more marginal characters, many of whom have sat with him in this room, trying to pretend they were legitimate players in the medical-cannabis trade.

"As a collective owner, you see a lot of vendors coming into your shop, trying to sell their medicine," Smith says. "When you sit down with them, you can glean a lot from them about who they are, where they come from, and what kind of operation they have . . . Now, I can't say I know specifically if this one guy is a Mexican cartel guy, but I can say that he's got gang tattoos, he can bring me one hundred pounds of brick medicine, and Mexican medicine is always bricked. You can draw *A* to *Z*."

Brick marijuana is cheap, outdoor weed grown in Mexico, then stuffed into bales compressed into dense bricks so that smuggling them across the border, either in a gas tank or on the back of a mule, becomes more efficient. "They come in our door and take a knife and cut a piece of it," Smith says. "And you look at the material, and it's completely patted down because that bale may have sat in a warehouse in Mexico for a month before it came north."

This kind of marijuana, explains Smith, doesn't begin to compete with the high-quality cannabis that currently lines the shelves of cannabis collectives in California and the other states, as well as the District of Columbia, that have legalized marijuana for medical use. "The strength is very weak, but the prices are very cheap. Nowadays, it goes into concentrated extracts or edibles, or it's sold under the name 'Train Wreck' or one of the other old-school names."

The fact that cheap Mexican weed is often sold under the name "Train Wreck" is an industry secret Smith says nobody in the marijuana business wants the general public to know. "There is no strain called Train Wreck," he claims. "Train Wreck is just what we call marginal weed. Nobody knows what it is." Then there's Purple Urkle. "Anybody can bring in some red buds with a little color to it and call it Purple Urkle or Jah OG," he says. "Anybody can bring in a dark bud and call it Hindu Kush. You'll never know. It's just a marketing tool."

Another secret, according to Smith: real marijuana doesn't look anything like what most people expect to see when they walk into their local dispensary. Those tight, dense buds that most stoners associate with the chronic look pretty and will get you high, but they've been shorn of their THC-laden leaves, either by hand-held trimmers or motorized tumblers. Sophisticated pot growers, including the cartels, are increasingly using those cheating tools to manufacture hash, kief, tinctures or edibles, thus potentially doubling their profit. "Nobody wants their customers to know that the hash and kief they're selling you came right from the buds sitting next to them on the same shelf," he says.

As Smith readily acknowledges, there are plenty of folks in the medical-marijuana community who wish he'd shut the hell up—and that's putting it mildly. In fact, Smith could be the most controversial person in California's medical marijuana community. Ever since he and his wife, Theresa, founded C3 in the living room of their Fullerton home seven years ago, his relationship with most other local activists and cannabis-club owners has gone from testy to bad to worse to, finally, all but nonexistent. He doesn't mind: in Smith's view, many of his competitors are really crooks.

"A lot of these guys who started these shops are pot dealers from the past," he claims, and immediately mentions Mark Moen—"He was just a drug dealer, selling pounds out the back door like any other," he says. "So I keep myself isolated. And within that isolation, I feel the security to say that commercial cultivators are stealing your medicine. They're selling you the nut and not the fruit; they're reselling the fruit to you and doubling their margins."

His critics, however, say Smith has an abrasive and self-righteous personality and has done more harm to the medical-marijuana movement than anyone else in the county. "Steele is one of the worst people I've ever been involved with," remarks one prominent activist. "He's delusional," claims another. "It's a shame," Kandice Hawes, president of the Orange County chapter of the National Organization for the Reform of Marijuana Laws (NORML), one of the largest and most active chapters in the country, tells me. "We don't want to be enemies of anyone, but Steele has repeatedly come into our group and caused problems. We want to work with him, and we want everything to be cool, but he keeps on attacking us, and he's kind of ruined the movement."

Besides, adds Hawes, "You'd think he'd want our help."

– – – – –

One thing is certain: few medical-marijuana activists have tempted fate as much has Steele Smith. His troubles began four years ago, when federal drug agents arrested him for illegal marijuana cultivation. Even while facing a trial that could have landed him in prison for years, he continued to openly distribute cannabis through his own storefront dispensary. The fact that he was able to do this without ever being rearrested says a lot about two things. First, there's the schizophrenic nature of medical marijuana's relationship with federal and state laws, in the sense that everything Smith is doing was more or less legal in California but illegal under federal law. Secondly, it says a lot about how careful Smith has been to distance himself from the likes of Moen and other dispensary operators who are foolhardy enough to drive around with large amounts of weed and/or cash in their own cars.

Meanwhile, to understand Smith's unyielding approach toward both law enforcement and his fellow marijuana activists, it helps to know a little bit about his pedigree. Smith's uncle, Leighton Hatch, was a California Supreme Court justice appointed by Ronald Reagan. Along with well-known drug-reform advocate and former Orange

County Superior Court Judge James P. Gray, both his parents—Dr. Clark Smith, a prominent Anaheim physician, and Katherine Smith, an Anaheim Union High School District board member—were signers of the 1993 Hoover Resolution, which called for a reform of US drug policy to focus less on incarceration and more on treatment and prevention.

Following four years at Anaheim's prestigious, private Servite High School, Smith graduated from the University of Southern California before attending Western State University College of Law. He married Theresa, and together they founded a marketing company for a product called ID Save, which fit around driver's licenses, preventing unwanted eyes from seeing people's addresses and other personal information. "My wife and I were able to eke out a small living and pay our bills," Smith says. "We had a nice little house. Life was good."

Everything changed a few weeks before September 11, 2001. Smith woke up one day feeling sick; sharp pains sliced through his stomach, making it impossible to eat. "I was sick and puking, and it got worse from there," he recalls. "I was going to the hospital every day. I went from seeing my own doctor to seeing gastrointestinal specialists and, finally, rare-diseases doctors."

One of those physicians happened to specialize in Zollinger-Ellison syndrome, a disease that causes ulcers of the duodenum, the first section of the lower intestine below the stomach. It took months to reach this diagnosis because of Smith's tall frame—most scopes were too short to reach all the way to his duodenum. It wasn't until a specialist noticed Smith's feet hanging well off the end of the surgical table that he realized why he couldn't find the telltale ulcers. "The guy rolls me on my side, which squishes my guts together, and into view came a field of ulcers—eleven of them," Smith says. "These ulcers are so painful they blind you. You can't see; you can't stand up. I dropped forty or forty-five pounds because I couldn't eat."

Doctors promptly put Smith on a regimen of powerful opiates. "They put him on major amounts of morphine, which we didn't even know was morphine because it was called Roxanol," says Theresa. "It came in a baby dropper," Smith adds. "It was so innocuous. And then two weeks later, I woke up at 4:00 AM, sweating. And this cold realization set in that this was detox, withdrawal." After more than a year on Roxanol, Smith realized he was addicted to the drug. He went through an experimental, rapid detoxification therapy. "It nearly killed him," Theresa recalls. "He had to go into the emergency room and was there for four days, and then he came out in a wheelchair."

In desperation, Smith turned to Suboxone, a drug that helps deal with the side effects of opium withdrawal, as well as medical marijuana, to ease the pain and nausea caused by the ever-present ulcers. In 2004, there were roughly twenty medical-marijuana dispensaries in Los Angeles and zero in Orange County. Smith and his wife soon grew tired of the lengthy freeway commute. "We figured that not only does Orange County need one of these clubs, but also that we can do this," Smith recalls. "We've been self-employed with our own business for fourteen years." Late that year, Smith and his wife formed C3—shorthand for California Compassionate Caregivers. "We opened it in our house in Fullerton, right there in the living room," Smith says. "We had patients coming into the house, and by the end of that first week, we had ten patients coming in a day."

In early 2005, the couple relocated to Placentia and rented a second-story apartment next to a restaurant. The apartment doubled as the location of the collective; beneath the unit was a secure garage where patients could park their cars. Smith also got involved with Orange County's burgeoning medical-marijuana-activist community. He claims he started the county's first chapter of Americans for Safe Access (ASA) out of the office of a Newport Beach lawyer friend of his, William Paoli. "We had a meeting once a night at this nice law firm," Smith recalls. "We had a good group of twenty-five, thirty patients showing up. The conference room was always full; we were standing room only. It was a very professional meeting. We didn't allow anyone to smoke out in the parking lot."

However, several prominent cannabis activists told me that Smith was exaggerating his role in ASA. "The first [ASA] meeting in my living room was five people" in 2004, says Tracy Neria, an OC NORML member who says she founded the local chapter. "Steele was never a board member or a member." Neria says she first met Smith a year later when she worked for a doctor who prescribed medical marijuana to patients, some of whom obtained their medicine from C3. "We'd had patients whom he delivered to who said he delivered moldy product," she says. "These were elderly patients. Our patients would call us, all upset, saying they were having problems with this guy. He was bringing them stuff they hadn't ordered, shorting them and being rude. They felt threatened by him."

At the time, Smith was growing his marijuana crop inside a two-thousand-square-foot house near Perris, on a ten-acre property surrounded by trees and nearly invisible from the outside. Smith hired another grower he knew to live at the house and run the day-to-day operations. But, Smith noticed as the first harvest came in months later, the crop perceptibly shrunk each time he visited. Suspicious, Smith asked an electrician friend to drop by, pretend to do work at the property, and then report what he saw. "The next day, he called and said, 'A green car just pulled up,'" he recalls. "'Two guys got out, and they've been inside ten minutes. They walked out with two brown paper bags, put them in the trunk and left.' He called back two hours later and said the same thing happened, this time with a minivan. So that was it. I knew I was being stolen from. I was done. It went to hell in a handbag."

In the early summer of 2007, before Smith had a chance to fire his foreman and harvest what was left of his crop, the police arrested the thief while he was away from the property. "He dropped a dime on the location, and the location got busted up by the police," he says. After the raid, Smith received a telephone call in Placentia from the Riverside County sheriff's department. "We looked into this property," a detective told him. "You signed the lease. Do you want to come out here and talk to us?" Smith said no. When the detective asked him to answer questions over the phone, Smith gave him the name of his attorney and hung up.

All Smith had left of his crop were the eighteen mother plants that had spawned the thousands of clones he was in the process of growing. With no place else to put them, he left them in the garage beneath his apartment. At about 7:00 PM on a Friday night, while hanging out with a friend, Smith heard a knock on the door. A bearded man wearing a chain of beads around his neck asked Smith if he was the owner of the Grand Cherokee that was parked in the alley. "I just clipped your mirror," the man said. "I'm really sorry."

When he reached the bottom of the stairs, two uniformed Placentia police officers confronted Smith and explained that while cruising down the alley, they'd noticed a garage door that hadn't been rolled all the way down; peering inside, they had seen Smith's plants. Smith told the cops he was a medical-marijuana patient and that the plants belonged to his collective. After spending several hours combing through his patient records, receipts, and other business and tax documents, the lead detective telephoned a prosecutor with the Orange County district attorney's office, who instructed the police to confiscate everything but make no arrests.

The detective also gave Smith his business card, along with instructions to call him in a few weeks about getting his property back. But when weeks passed and none of his calls were returned, Smith grew impatient. He hired Paoli to file a civil suit against the city of Placentia. Meanwhile, Smith and his wife moved back to Fullerton. There, in July 2007, police visited two houses where Smith was in the process of cultivating approximately four thousand plants for the collective, which had just opened its new headquarters in Garden Grove. This time, despite the high number of plants, the cops not only made no arrests, but they also left without seizing any property. Smith even claims a female captain told him she'd never seen a collective with as much paperwork as his and to call her if he ever had problems with the city. He wasn't as lucky a few months later, when the Smiths awoke at about 4:00 AM to the sound of their front door being knocked down.

A squad of federal drug-enforcement agents entered the house, spraying fire extinguishers inside to create a disorienting fog so that for a moment, all Smith saw were red laser lights and shadows of what looked like paramilitary forces. Other Drug Enforcement Administration (DEA) units simultaneously raided his two Fullerton grow houses, as well as C3's Garden Grove headquarters, confiscating no fewer than 3,860 marijuana plants. Both Smith and his wife were arrested and charged with illegally cultivating marijuana. Also arrested that morning were Alex Valentine and Dennis Leland. Valentine, a twenty-one-year-old member of C3 who suffers from von Recklinghausen's disease, was staying at one of the grow houses; Leland was a homeless friend of a friend whom the Smiths had allowed to sleep at another house in return for helping with minor chores. Because of Smith's medical condition, he wasn't housed at the Theo Lacy Jail in Orange, where most local federal inmates are held awaiting trial, but rather at the Metropolitan Detention Center in downtown Los Angeles.

Although his wife was released on bail after two months—they were housed on different floors but were able to shout at each other through air ducts once or twice a day until weekly visits could be arranged—Smith spent ten months in jail. Among other things, he survived a massive race riot that began on his floor and spread throughout the facility, leading to several days of lockdown, and became addicted once again to painkillers, specifically Oxycontin, which was prescribed to him by jail doctors for his ulcers. After being released, Smith spent a year on house arrest with an ankle monitoring bracelet and gradually weaned himself off opiates with copious amounts of medical marijuana.

During his incarceration, Smith says, rivals within the Orange County ASA chapter had taken over the weekly meetings at Paoli's law office in Newport Beach, which he claims began to deteriorate. "They weren't respecting the rules I had in place," he says. "People were smoking in the parking lot, and the neighbors complained to the senior partner, who told Bill he had to get those people out of there."

ASA began to hold its meetings at a pizza parlor where the OCNORML meetings were held. Smith showed up at one of the meetings, insisted the two groups should meet separately, and announced he was running for president of ASA. In Smith's view, one that is in fact shared by many activists, the two organizations have separate and mutually exclusive goals: while ASA advocates for medical-cannabis patients, NORML's mission is to push authorities to legalize marijuana. Hence, he argued, the two groups had no business sharing meetings or members. "When I said that, it pissed off that whole group," Smith says.

"Steele just stood up and said he was having elections and nominated himself president out of the blue," says Marla James, a paraplegic who unsuccessfully sued Dana Point and Costa Mesa for violating the Americans with Disabilities Act by banning marijuana dispensaries and who now heads Orange County's ASA chapter. "He hadn't been to a single meeting in the past year, so I told him he couldn't run, according to our bylaws, and he hadn't paid any dues and wasn't on the membership list. So then he demanded the membership list and sent me all kinds of e-mails and left threatening messages on my voice mail. He threatened to sue me, and it was really as if he had a psychiatric break."

James says she often wonders if Smith's painful medical symptoms might explain at least some of the personality conflict. "I've tried to understand him for a long time," she says. "My opinion is he needs medication more than cannabis. He is a very charming man, but what's sad is that his wife, Theresa, who is a wonderful lady, was arrested, too, but if you look on his website, it just says, 'Steele's Case' and doesn't mention Theresa or the other people arrested who could go to prison. It's just like the whole world is centered on him, so I choose not to be in his world—a lot of people choose that. He's made a lot of enemies."

One of those enemies is Joe Grumbine, former owner of two Long Beach collectives and the Unit D collective in Garden Grove, who is also the director of the medical-marijuana activist group the Human Solution, which travels up and down the state providing courtroom support for California dispensary operators brought up on charges of selling pot (including Grumbine's own felony pot case—more on that later). Grumbine said he still remembers the first time he met Smith. "He came into my collective and didn't have his paperwork," Grumbine recalls. "My people are trained to not let people come in without a [doctor's note]. He came back with an expired note, and we called the doctor to see if it was valid, and he said it wasn't, so we said, 'You can't come in.' I didn't see him much after that."

Later, Grumbine learned that Smith was spreading rumors that Grumbine, who is viewed as a hero by many medical-marijuana activists for his social work through the Human Solution—including the distribution of free marijuana to low-income and disabled patients—was really a "drug dealer" masquerading as a humanitarian. "He is a very toxic person to our movement," Grumbine says. "I don't even have a collective anymore, and all my resources were taken from me. If I'm a drug dealer, then why am I still fighting for other people's rights?"

Despite believing that Smith has tried to sully his reputation behind his back, Grumbine says he's made a point of showing up in court to support Smith in his pretrial hearings, a favor that Smith has so far declined to return. "Me and a handful of guys were the only people present at his last hearing," Grumbine recalls. "My philosophy and belief is that that nobody should go to jail for a plant. Regardless of my opinion [of] someone, if they are a jerk or not socially adept, I would always be supportive. That said, he's never done anything for anybody, and if you're not on his show, you're nobody."

After falling out with James and her ASA group, Smith started his own chapter. "I basically said, 'Forget it; you guys can have that group,'" Smith recalls. "I'm gonna take my ASA to a new address, and you can do what you want." Smith also formed a trade organization called the Greater Orange County Collective Alliance (GOCCA), which he claims represents the most ethical cannabis collectives in the county. To join the group, collectives must go through what Smith describes as a rigorous accreditation process and hand over to him all their corporate paperwork proving they comply with state law and operate at the highest professional standards.

So far, however, only six collectives have joined GOCCA. To Smith, that simply proves his thesis that many collectives are actually just "front groups" for drug dealers. "Six collectives is about 10 percent of the total number of collectives in the county," he estimates. "Those 10 percent really represent the cream of the crop. The other 90 percent wants to remain in the shadows, doing the gray things that they do just to make some money. They don't want to be in the spotlight of the city or the police, so they operate off the board." (Eventually, both feds and police would shut down most of the marijuana dispensaries in California, including Orange County, including a few members of GOCCA, and at press time, Smith's was one of the last ones still open.)

Meanwhile, after numerous delays, Smith still faces a federal marijuana-cultivation case, although all charges were dismissed against his wife. If it goes to trial, it will become the first federal case in the nation in which a defendant will be able to mention the words "medical marijuana." Previously, juries in such cases had no way of knowing if the defendant was a sick patient growing medicine for his or her collective or a garden-variety weed farmer. But as Smith's own defense attorney, Eric Shevin, points out, there is still no "medical marijuana" defense to marijuana cultivation in federal law.

In other words, Smith's only hope at a not-guilty verdict is a sympathetic jury deliberately ignoring this fact, despite the judge's inevitable instructions to the contrary. Besides, Shevin adds, prosecutors have repeatedly offered Smith a settlement the attorney described as "too good to refuse." So far, however, his client has refused to cop a plea. "To hope a jury acquits you just because they hear the words 'medical marijuana' is super risky," Shevin says. "To fight this case and be a martyr just to be heard? The stakes are just incredibly high."

For his part, Smith seems incredibly unworried about his legal prospects. He points out that Shevin has filed motions in his case arguing the federal government has no right to penalize conduct that is legal under state laws. "The government doesn't want to answer those motions," Smith says. "I will probably get a favorable judgment. There are fifteen other states watching this, and if I win, there will be a new law that all those states can use."

If Smith wins in federal court, he'll also regain his legal standing to sue the city of Placentia, which he believes is responsible for setting in motion the ordeal of the past several years of his life. Thanks to the ten months of incarceration he suffered after he filed the original lawsuit, he says with almost giddy excitement, the amount of damages he can claim has risen exponentially.

"The attorneys I'm talking to say the sky's the limit," Smith enthuses, adding that unlike Mark Moen, he doesn't have any prior convictions and no previous drug record.

"I went to USC," he boasts. "I went to law school. I'm a seventh-generation Californian. I'm a patient. I've got a rare disease.

"Fuck—I'm the perfect storm!"

5 | The Two Joes

Joe Grumbine is in Egg Heaven.

The Long Beach eatery is one of the city's most celebrated diners, the only downside being that it's a cash-only joint. It first opened back in 1969, and its existence in this particular neighborhood is something of an anomaly. Long Beach is just about the grittiest coastal city in California, with the possible exception of Oakland. On the one hand, the city is famous for gangster rappers like Snoop Dogg and punk-ska bands such as Sublime that have done much to popularize marijuana in American culture. But the city is half inner city and half white, upper-middle-class suburb, and Egg Heaven Cafe, with its greasy-spoon menu and cash-paying customer base, is a stubbornly retrograde outpost in the increasingly trendy, upscale enclave of Belmont Heights.

The restaurant has been the main source of income of Grumbine's friend and business partner Joe Byron for the past seventeen years. Right now, on this spring day in 2011, the two Joes are sitting on opposite sides of a booth table. Byron is well over six feet tall, with a ruddy complexion and dark hair. He looks every bit the businessman.

Grumbine is shorter, with wavy, shoulder-length hair, and is wearing a billowy, white, button-down shirt that has a green ribbon with a red cross pinned to it, the symbol of his medical-marijuana activist group, the Human Solution.

Both men poke at their eggs as they struggle to make sense of being prosecuted for something that, while apparently illegal for them to do, isn't illegal for a bunch of other people to do. That, at least, seems to be at the center of the Kafkaesque riddle that has become their lives, one that tends to put a dent in one's appetite and makes one's brain hurt even if one has already downed a few cups of strong coffee.

The two Joes are facing trial at the Long Beach Courthouse of Los Angeles Superior Court for dispensing medical marijuana to members of their cannabis collective—that is, they sold the pot to qualified patients who showed up at their storefront and presented valid California driver's licenses and legitimate recommendations from licensed physicians stating they were medical-marijuana patients whose right to obtain and smoke cannabis is protected under state law. The only problem: the patients in question turned out to be undercover police officers who were part of a major operation aimed at taking Byron and Grumbine out of the medical-marijuana trade and sending them to prison. If convicted of selling marijuana, each man will face seven years in state prison.

On its face, the case is a bit anachronistic. It's been fifteen years since California voters overwhelmingly passed Proposition 215, legalizing marijuana for state residents with a legitimate doctor's recommendation, and there's no evidence Byron or Grumbine "sold" pot to anyone who didn't fit that description. And in November 2010, a majority of Long Beach residents voted to support Proposition 19, the failed state initiative that would have legalized marijuana for recreational use, and a whopping 73 percent of city residents voted in favor of a municipal measure to tax the dozens of marijuana dispensaries operating within the city. Meanwhile, unlike Mark Moen, neither Byron nor Grumbine were caught red-handed with hundreds of thousands of dollars in cash or a trunk full of recently harvested Emerald Triangle weed.

All that's a bit beside the point, however. Dispensing marijuana isn't just legal under state law; it also happens to be an activity that the city of Long Beach has since endorsed by passing an ordinance allowing cannabis collectives to operate within the city. In fact, Long Beach has already accepted applications to receive legal permits from dozens of marijuana dispensaries that are already doing exactly what Byron and Grumbine are about to be prosecuted for doing. Both men are quick to point out this fact, and two others: until their December 17, 2009, arrests, neither of them had ever been in trouble with the law, and they were both upstanding members of Long Beach's business community.

"How many times have you been to jail, Joe?" Byron asks his friend, theatrically turning his head back and forth to see how many people at nearby tables might be overhearing the conversation.

"Zero," Grumbine says.

Then Grumbine corrects himself: he was arrested on December 10, 2008, when a Riverside County Sheriff's deputy pulled him over a few miles from his house near Perris and found ten pounds of marijuana in his trunk. The pot, he told the deputy, belonged to his cannabis collective in Garden Grove, Unit D. "We had just opened up the collective and didn't have all the security features we have now," Grumbine explains. "We couldn't afford it, so every night, one of us took the medicine home." He spent the night in jail; the charges were later dropped.

"How about you, Joe?" Grumbine asks Byron. "How many times have you been to jail?"

"Zero," Byron responds, wistfully shaking his head. A moment of silence follows.

"Yeah," he adds.

– – – – –

Byron and Grumbine's haphazard descent from legitimate business-men to high-profile defendants in the city's schizophrenic war on weed began on New Year's Eve 2000. That's when the two childhood friends grabbed a couple of beers and sat on a pair of paint buckets in Grumbine's garage, gearing up for a brainstorming session. They had a lot in common—and not in a good way: both men were not only broke, but also heavily in debt, facing imminent financial doom.

Grumbine, a housepainter who grew up in Fullerton, was living in a house near Perris, where he'd turned a dirty hillside into a botanical garden that hosted weddings—until Riverside County shut him down for violating a zoning ordinance. He'd spent thousands of dollars in legal fees fighting the county, but he lost, had to return fifty deposits on future ceremonies, and had no new cash coming in. Byron, raised next door to northern Orange County in Whittier, was also struggling financially. Although Egg Heaven, which he has now owned for seventeen years, was doing well, he'd just lost the lease on a pub in Long Beach. "Egg Heaven didn't pay all the bills," Byron says. "So I talked to Joe and told him I had a plan that could work for both of us."

By the time the two had finished their beers, they'd agreed to open a real-estate brokerage firm that could hopefully reverse their mutual financial misfortune courtesy of Southern California's ever-expanding housing bubble. They formed Mission Priority Lending, a boutique mortgage broker in Long Beach's upscale Belmont Shore peninsula. Business boomed for a while, but in 2007, the housing market imploded in Southern California and throughout the United

States. For more than half a year, the pair struggled to keep afloat, but by the summer of 2008, as the global economy itself began to tank, it was clear they needed to switch careers. Suddenly, the two Joes were back where they started, minus the paint buckets.

But just when it seemed like both men were headed to the poorhouse, rumors circulated around town that the Long Beach city council, unlike many other municipal bodies in California, was going to issue permits to marijuana collectives operating in the city. Like any entrepreneurs, Byron and Grumbine wanted to capitalize on the opportunity. Over the next year they opened a trio of dispensaries, two in Long Beach and one in Garden Grove. In retrospect, everything would've been fine if Byron and Grumbine had ignored the positive vibes coming out of Long Beach City Hall and just stayed in Orange County. After opening their Unit D cannabis collective in Garden Grove in March 2008, the two men had their share of visits from the local cops—but they were all of the friendly, you're-not-under-arrest variety.

"They stopped by maybe half a dozen times," Byron recalls. "First, they inspected us with code enforcement; then they came in a couple of months later and said, 'We have a new guy on the beat here.'"

Garden Grove's finest asked Byron and Grumbine to show them how to tell the difference between a legitimate doctor's recommendation for cannabis and something a stoner might fake on his computer. "We told the cops what we do and what to look for," Byron says. "A few months later, a new cop shows up, says, 'I do traffic stops all the time; I smell pot, and they hand me a piece of paper. Can you help me?' They were really friendly to us."

Unlike other dispensaries, Unit D did a lot more than distribute marijuana. They also gave out free clothing, food, and medicine to low-income patients, as well as wheelchairs to disabled members of the collective. Central to that effort was Charles Monson, director of the nonprofit group Wheels of Mercy. When Monson was arrested in October 2007 for growing marijuana, his lawyer asked him to stop cultivating until the case was settled. That's how he met Byron and Grumbine.

"I needed a way to get my medicine," says Monson, a quadriplegic who broke his neck in a Newport Beach swimming accident when he was sixteen. Since he lives on a fixed income and couldn't afford the cannabis, he offered to provide Unit D with services in exchange for his medicine. "I taught classes on how to cook with medicine, made sure people got wheelchairs who needed them, created a program in which we put grab rails in people's homes."

Byron and Grumbine assisted in the fieldwork. "If one of our members needed a wheelchair ramp, we'd go and build it for him," Byron says. "We loved doing that. If someone needed something, we'd go and do what needed to be done. It was a lot of fun."

In return, members would donate food and clothing to the collective. "We had one guy who always brought in loads of fresh bread," Byron says. "We were running it as an actual collective, the way you are supposed to do it. It wasn't some party situation, with guys in dreadlocks and people smoking medicine on-site or with a hookah in the backyard."

At first, Long Beach seemed just as friendly as Garden Grove when it came to medical marijuana. "I knew the city [was] getting ready with rules and regulations on licensing medical marijuana," Byron says. "We went to all the city council meetings. We called city hall a couple of times and went down there because we knew there were dispensaries in town." They soon found the city wasn't yet issuing permits for dispensaries, but it had already begun drafting an ordinance that would open the way for that process to begin.

With that in mind, Byron and Grumbine rented a shop at the intersection of Fourth and Elm Streets in downtown Long Beach and another off Lakewood Boulevard. Shortly after they opened for business, they received a telephone call from the Los Angeles County district attorney's office. "The DA's office called us just to see who we were and what we were doing. They said, 'Don't worry about the phone call,'" Byron recalls. "'We're just finding out where everybody is, and when this license thing goes through, we'll be able to contact you then.'"

Unlike many marijuana dispensaries that had stoner-friendly monikers such as 420 and After Midnight, Byron and Grumbine chose nondescript, address-specific names for their Long Beach locations: Fourth and Elm Natural Health Collective and the 2200 Health Collective. "We opened Fourth and Elm first," Byron says. "We thought we'd need a bunch of locations because we figured that once the ordinance passed, maybe one of those locations wouldn't work."

When the city announced its proposed ordinance would require each dispensary to grow its own cannabis, Byron and Grumbine rented a cultivation space off Long Beach Boulevard and also began growing at the Fourth and Elm dispensary. "We didn't sell or distribute out of the [Long Beach Boulevard] location," Byron says. "We were just going to use it as a facility to grow medicine. We were probably there about three or four months before the raid."

— — — — —

On December 17, 2009, Byron was just putting the finishing touches on the air-conditioning system at their cultivation warehouse when several Long Beach police officers in SWAT gear, with their guns drawn, burst through the doors and arrested him. Simultaneously, police raided Unit D in Garden Grove, where Grumbine was working, as well as his house in Perris, where officers knocked down a gate and arrested his wife and nineteen-year-old daughter at gunpoint. "I opened the door with a gun to my head," Grumbine recalls.

"I stared down the barrel of a nine millimeter and said, 'I guess I'm putting my hands up.'"

That day, cops also raided the homes of Byron and Grumbine's seventeen employees, all of whom were arrested and sent to the Long Beach Jail; there, they were subjected to full-cavity body searches and put in holding cells overnight before being released with no charges filed. "I was thrown into a dingy dungeon and told to bend over and cough," says Katherine Hamill, who was working the front office at Unit D on the day of the raid. "I'm not a criminal. I had never been arrested in my life. It was the most degrading thing. I was bawling; it was so wrong."

Paul LaFond, manager of the Fourth and Elm collective, was filling in for an employee who was running late that morning when the police arrived. "Right at 11:00 AM, about twelve police officers came in and immediately put me in handcuffs," LaFond recalls. "And within about three or four minutes, I was put in a car and taken to my house, where I was read my rights." Police ransacked the house, LaFond claims, and even refused to help his elderly housemate and landlord walk down the hall to get out of the way. "He was holding onto the wall, trying to keep his balance," he says. "I would have gotten up and helped him, but I was handcuffed."

As it soon became obvious, Long Beach police had placed Byron and Grumbine's three dispensaries, including Garden Grove's Unit D, as well as the grow house, under surveillance weeks earlier. They'd sent in several plainclothes police officers who'd purchased medical marijuana after having their doctor's notes verified, as required by state law, each time. It later was revealed that the cops had an informant helping them, a disgruntled employee who'd been fired by Grumbine for drinking on the job. An affidavit used in the raid cited claims he made that Byron and Grumbine were hoarding cash from pot sales and disguising the club's day-to-day operations to make it appear that less money was going through the dispensary. Presumably, the police figured they were taking down a major dope-dealing operation run by a pair of profiteers. But unlike similar raids, such as the one against Mark Moen of the now-defunct 215 Agenda that netted hundreds of thousands of dollars, police managed to seize only about $35,000 from Byron and Grumbine's operation.

Although police failed to file charges against anyone arrested in the raid, Byron and Grumbine were both rearrested more than a year later, on December 8, 2010. Prosecutor Jodi Castano claimed at the time and throughout the two men's subsequent criminal trial that both men were simple pot dealers. She also repeatedly expressed the view that state law prohibited storefront dispensaries from operating, and that sick Californians might be entitled to collectively grow cannabis, but once money started changing hands— "donations," in the parlance of the dispensaries—the law was being violated. Thus Byron and Grumbine's prosecution became a test case for the limits of the medical-marijuana business model. If they could be successfully prosecuted and sent to prison for selling pot, then any other dispensary operator could face the same penalty— and not from federal law enforcement officials citing pot's illicit nature under US law, but by state and local authorities.

In fact, the timing of the two men's arrest and arraignment on pot-sales charges in December 2010 coincided with Los Angeles District Attorney Steve Cooley's declaration of war against L.A. County's legions of pot clubs. Although Los Angeles had long tolerated medical-marijuana dispensaries, by 2010, hundreds of clubs were open for business, their green-cross-designated storefronts sprouting up by the dozens along industrial streets throughout the city and county, with attractive young females in nurses outfits handing out flyers for dispensaries and doctor referral services along the tourist-friendly Venice Beach boardwalk. Cooley clearly had had enough of them, which is why he helped author the official ballot argument against Proposition 19, which narrowly lost at the polls a month before Byron and Grumbine were officially charged. Prop. 19, Cooley claimed, was "flawed public policy and would compromise the safety of [California's] roadways, workplaces, and communities."

Together, Byron and Grumbine were charged with eighteen felony counts of selling marijuana, plus other charges stemming from the raid. Separately, Byron was also charged with failing to pay taxes on the marijuana sold at the dispensaries (he argues that paying taxes on marijuana sales hasn't protected others from being prosecuted for selling pot) and for stealing a fraction of the electrical power the club was using at the Fourth and Elm location from SoCal Edison. Byron insists a contractor he hired to do the wiring for the dispensary inadvertently connected a few outlets to the wrong power source.

As Byron and Grumbine finish up their breakfast at Egg Heaven, they reflect on the fact they've rejected repeated offers by prosecutors to settle the case before trial, a deal they claim would involve no further jail time. So far, they've refused because they don't want to plead guilty to felonies for doing something they don't believe is wrong.

"I've got American blood going back before the Revolutionary War," Grumbine says. "I was born an American citizen, and I value that and all the rights that have been given to me, and if I plead guilty to a felony, I lose a lot of those."

"We thought about taking a deal, but it just wouldn't be the right thing to do," adds Byron. "Maybe if the city apologizes and drops the charges to a misdemeanor."

That said, both men admit prosecutors have not only a strong case that they are guilty of dispensing marijuana, but an ironclad one at that. "There is no question that we had marijuana and were dispensing it," Grumbine explains. "We're just saying we were doing that within the confines of the law. I look at the charges against us, and there is no basis for any of it. It's a fucking joke."

"You know," Byron interjects in a hushed voice, "what's really funny is there's a guy with the DA's office sitting right behind us."

Everyone at the table turns around to see a middle-aged man with an olive complexion and slicked-back hair in a yellow shirt and tie, reading a newspaper. It's unclear if the man has been eavesdropping on the entire conversation, or if he is just enjoying his eggs. Either way, the narc knows he's been caught, and starts eating faster.

"Surf's up," he says.

– – – – –

Several months later, I'm sitting in the sixth-floor courtroom of Long Beach Superior Court Judge Charles D. Sheldon, a seventy-nine-year-old jurist with white hair, a bushy mustache, and a gravelly voice reminiscent of a *True Grit*–era John Wayne. On the wall next to the entrance to Sheldon's courtroom is a placard that reads DEPARTMENT K. That letter, as another Long Beach judge once drew unintended laughs for explaining, stands for that lovable, bouncy rodent from Down Under: the kangaroo. The joke being that in Sheldon's courtroom, all defendants are presumed guilty until sent to jail or prison: a kangaroo court for the war on medical marijuana.

It'd be funny if it weren't true.

Sheldon's intense dislike of Joe Byron and Joe Grumbine and their lawyers, Allison Margolin and Christopher Glew, became obvious early in the case through the judge's pretrial rulings. Margolin is a young and attractive lawyer whose father, Bruce Margolin, is a famous crusading attorney for marijuana rights who served as director of the L.A. chapter of NORML for twenty-nine years. Unlike Glew, who carries himself with supreme confidence in the courtroom, almost but crucially not quite to the point of arrogance, Alison Margolin seems at first blush to be a little scatterbrained. On a typical day in Sheldon's courtroom, she's fumbling for the right paperwork, begging hizzoner's pardon, pushing her eyeglasses back up on her nose, and mumbling to herself. At first Sheldon seems to find her somewhat amusing, but he quickly turns mean and lets his exasperation show in front of the jury.

It didn't help matters much, meanwhile, that every day, a couple dozen of the two Joes' supporters, members of the Human Solution, dutifully filed into court wearing their red-cross-on-a-green ribbon pendants pinned to their shirts. Shuffled might be a better word, however. Most of the supporters were elderly, handicapped, or both. One of them, Marla James, the president of the Orange County chapter of Americans for Safe Access, is missing the lower part of one of her legs and therefore had to be ushered into the courtroom in a wheelchair.

Others in the crowd were less sympathetic-looking. They had long hair, and some even had dreadlocks, the kind that white hippies furiously cultivate: unwashed, twisted knots of hair stuffed into Rastafarian knit hats. By and large, they reeked of a mixture of patchouli and freshly smoked weed. They were, in other words, more or less the equivalent of the lawn section of a Grateful Dead show. Occasionally, one of their cell phones would go off and the person would be ejected from the courtroom, muttering about how it was a conspiracy by the corrupt Long Beach police to keep them from bearing witness. To their credit, the bailiffs mostly left the audience members alone, although they did repeatedly threaten to kick anyone out who huffed aloud their general disapproval of the entire case.

The trial went badly for the two Joes even before it began, when Sheldon denied the defendants the right to mention the phrase "medical marijuana" in their defense, much less the fact that California state law allows patients to smoke marijuana for medical reasons and establish collectives to grow and distribute the plants. Only a last-minute ruling by the California Court of Appeal forced Sheldon to allow such a defense. Once Sheldon's ruling was overturned, the judge immediately refused a motion by the defense team to delay the trial for a week so the lawyers could restructure their case and contact previously off-limits witnesses, gruffly insisting the trial start the following morning. Things only got worse from there. When the prosecution argued its case, Sheldon denied almost every defense objection, and he allowed prosecutors to put more than thirty witnesses on the stand. He later limited each defendant to exactly six witnesses each.

Despite the lopsided nature of the proceedings, the prosecution didn't really amount to much—at least in terms of actual crimes. In its essence, the case boiled down to a dozen supposed "sales" made to undercover police officers who admitted to the jury they weren't allowed inside the club until they could provide a valid California driver's license and a doctor's note allowing them to smoke marijuana for medical reasons.

Given that state law allowed the cops to obtain those doctors' notes and to obtain cannabis to treat their supposed ailment—insomnia, as one cop sarcastically informed the jury—it was hard to see exactly where a crime had occurred. Indeed, the defendants happily acknowledged the so-called sales had taken place, but, they pointed out, their cash-strapped patients were habitually handed free cannabis; food drives and wheelchair donations were common events, and Grumbine drove to disabled patients' homes to help them cultivate their own marijuana, even installing wheelchair ramps and grab bars at their houses.

The evidence for any compelling crime may have been underwhelming, but the courtroom drama was anything but forgettable. For reasons only he knows, but which the California Commission on Judicial Performance might be well advised to contemplate, Sheldon allowed prosecutors to place a screen on the left side of the courtroom. This effectively blocked the jury from seeing the audience, which consisted overwhelmingly of current and former patients of the three collectives, mostly elderly people and folks in wheelchairs. At one point, frustrations at the defense table got the better of them, and a juror handed Sheldon a note asking him to admonish Glew and Margolin to not roll their eyes. On another occasion, citing Sheldon's bias, Glew attempted to argue for a mistrial; Sheldon responded by declaring a break in the proceedings. In full view of the jury, he took off his robe and began to march out of the courtroom. "Your honor, if I could just finish my sentence," Glew said.

Sheldon became enraged. "We're not talking about this," he bellowed, jabbing his finger in the air as he stormed out. "You're out of line!"

Later, Sheldon interrupted a clearly intimidated Margolin to tell her that she was doing a "disservice" to her clients by objecting too frequently, warning her that any further attempts would be futile. When Margolin protested, Sheldon cut her off. "You'll make your objections, and I'll overrule them," he snarled.

When it came time for Margolin and Glew to present their case, Sheldon seemed to have much more interest in sustaining objections, seeing as they were now coming from the prosecution table. This trend continued well into closing arguments, when Sheldon overruled each defense objection during prosecutor Castano's speech. For example, when Castano told the jury the law doesn't allow for collectives to sell marijuana at a profit nor does it provide for patients to obtain cannabis via over-the-counter sales, Margolin repeatedly objected on the grounds the statement misstated the law, but Sheldon repeatedly ignored her.

When Castano objected roughly half a dozen times to Margolin's closing speech on the same grounds, Sheldon repeatedly sustained her objections, referring to Margolin's arguments as "improper" and ruling they be stricken from the record. In fact, Sheldon had to ask the courtroom reporter to read back Margolin's statements each time Castano objected because he wasn't even listening to Margolin's speech. Typically, judges avoid this kind of intervention by simply reminding the jury that nothing the attorneys say during closing arguments should be considered as evidence, but Sheldon either forgot to say this or didn't see the point.

Speaking of forgetfulness, during more than a week of courtroom proceedings, Sheldon never admonished jurors to not speak about the case with one another or anyone else—an amazing oversight. Because of a gag rule Sheldon imposed on the lawyers in the case, Glew, Margolin, and Castano were prohibited from speaking with reporters. But speaking in the hallway shortly before the trial ended, Grumbine laughed nervously as he tried to make sense of the case. "It's a personal vendetta or something," he concluded. "Maybe it's just a dream, or we stepped into an alternate reality."

– – – – –

The jury began deliberating on December 20, 2011. Late in the morning the following day, they reached a verdict: guilty on all counts. In explaining the verdict, an anonymous juror pointed to their belief that Byron and Grumbine had failed to pay enough taxes to cover the amount of sales they believed Unit D was making each month. Because the defense had failed to provide convincing paperwork showing where all the cash went at the end of each day, the juror added, it was reasonable to assume that both men were pocketing the proceeds. The fact that, at trial, no evidence surfaced of large amounts of cash being pocketed by either man, much less being funneled into large purchases such as a new house or car, apparently didn't sway the verdict. Mercifully, however, both Byron and Grumbine were allowed to stay out of jail over the holidays. Then a strange thing happened. On January 11, 2012, the day the two defendants were supposed to be sentenced, Sheldon—channeling Lyndon B. Johnson in his famous 1968 speech when he announced he would not seek nor would he accept a nomination to run for a second term as president—announced he was removing himself from the case.

First Sheldon attempted to deny he'd ever been unfair. "The court is not biased in favor of any party or counsel," he asserted, in response to the latest recusal motion by defense attorneys Glew and Margolin, which included a laundry list of his objectionable statements. However, Sheldon acknowledged that he hadn't helped his case by sending a January 4 letter to Sally Thomas, head deputy of the Long Beach branch of the Los Angeles district attorney's office, in which he offered glowing praise for prosecutor Jodi Castano.

"Frankly, I made a mistake," Sheldon observed. "I wasn't thinking when I sent a commendatory letter to the district attorney." That said, Sheldon quickly added, "I meant what I said in the letter."

In the letter, Sheldon stated that he couldn't remember the last time he was "moved to writing a letter commending" a prosecutor but that he was "moved to do so" in this case. "Ms. Castano, despite operating in the courtroom, often full or almost full of persons overtly favoring the defense side, was unflappable, composed, steady, organized, and totally professional from beginning to end," Sheldon wrote. Her "extraordinary preparation and excellent meticulous and painstaking presentation of evidence was a pleasure to observe. . . . In short, I just want you to know you chose the right lawyer to handle this difficult case."

Glew and Margolin had already prepared a motion to disqualify Sheldon before they had gotten wind of his letter. After Sheldon recused himself, Glew asked if this meant that Sheldon's previous gag order against speaking to the media was now lifted. "I'm not making any other orders because of what I just said," Sheldon responded. "I'm off the case."

Three months later, on April 13, 2012, acting on a motion for a new trial by Glew and Margolin, Long Beach Superior Court Judge Joan Comparet-Cassani threw out the two men's convictions, awarding them the right to a new and hopefully fair trial. In making her ruling, Comparet-Cassani referred to several aspects of Sheldon's mishandling of the case. For example, Comparet-Cassani argued, Sheldon complimented Castano, in front of jurors, while also being so rude to the defense team that he actually brought Margolin to tears at one point when jurors were about to enter the room. Instead of giving Margolin a few minutes to collect herself, Comparet-Cassani noted, Sheldon allowed the jurors to march into court.

Comparet-Cassani observed that Sheldon also ruled that a videotape and a photograph were relevant to the prosecution's case and should therefore be allowed into evidence—without ever having examined the video or photograph in question. Just as questionable to Comparet-Cassani was the fact that trial transcripts show that while Sheldon sustained the vast majority of the prosecution's objections, it wasn't until page 1,004 of the transcripts that Sheldon sustained a defense objection. The judge described Sheldon's actions as a series of errors that began before the trial even started, and which continued and worsened over the course of the proceedings. She noted that before the trial began Sheldon sought to deny Byron or Grumbine the right to even mention medical marijuana, and then, when another judge overturned his ruling, he forced the defense to go to trial the very next day.

"This was a terrible, terrible, terrible trial," Comparet-Cassani concluded.

Her ruling, which overturned a pair of criminal verdicts in a case supervised by a fellow judge even before the verdicts were formally appealed, is relatively rare, Glew told me. "To have a hearing like this—and to have the motion for a new trial actually get granted—is very rare. And the only reason it happened is because Sheldon recused himself from trial."

"For today, justice prevailed," a delighted Margolin announced in the hallway a few moments after the hearing ended.

"We couldn't be happier with today's result," Glew added, triumphantly. "I'll just echo [Comparet-Cassani's] sentiments. This was a terrible trial."

But the trial wasn't just a terrible miscarriage of justice because of a bad judge. Amazingly, by the time the Los Angeles County district attorney's office got around to hauling Byron and Grumbine into court, the city of Long Beach had already enacted a medical-marijuana ordinance that officially sanctioned the operation of similarly run cannabis clubs within city limits. I'd eventually discover that the entire process was fraught with enough incompetence and corruption to warrant an FBI investigation. For the two Joes, however, the very existence of such a process was inexplicable.

The most outrageous aspect of the whole charade is the fact that the city actually granted preliminary approval to two dispensaries that opened their doors at the exact same addresses where Byron and Grumbine's collectives were located. Replacing their planned marijuana-cultivation center (the city required that all collectives grow their product within city limits) is one run by an outfit calling itself the NLB Collective. Another address where Byron and Grumbine were planning to grow marijuana is now being operated by an organization called the Airport Collective.

As for the collective that Byron and Grumbine were running off Lakewood Boulevard? That address was taken over by a dispensary called the Industry Green Collective, which is next door to a cultivation center run by the same collective. "All these clubs are doing exactly what my client was charged with doing," Glew told me. "And what's crazier than that is the fact that it's actually being condoned by the city of Long Beach. The whole thing is just surreal."

6 | Rock Bottom

I didn't have to travel far from the courthouse where the two Joes were tried to figure out that the entire trial was a complete mockery of justice.

To be exact, I only had to drive about half a mile, to the Avalon Wellness Collective, which, except for the oversized green cross painted on the wall and the acrylic sign with the olive-colored marijuana seed inside the letter O, looked exactly like all the other razor-wire-topped, one-story buildings that line the west side of the 710 freeway. The front door, which had just been carved into the front of the building, opens to reveal a burly guard sitting on a stool. Behind him, another security door opened to what turns out to be a "man trap": once the first door closes, visitors are locked inside a chamber until they're buzzed through.

Beyond that, in the actual dispensary area, jars of organic medicine previously tested for pesticides, mold, and E. coli were neatly arranged inside a glass-topped display case. A flat-screen television stretched across one wall, and watching everything from a ceiling corner is a tilt-pan, zoom-lens security camera. In the summer of 2011, the eight-thousand-square-foot charcoal-gray building, located in an industrial neighborhood of north-central Long Beach, was just an empty warehouse; now, just six months later, a state-of-the-art, one-stop cannabis cultivation-and-distribution center operates inside, built to exacting city specifications.

Nearly half the sprawling structure is divided between a vegetation area, a hydroponics setup, and a large worktable at which several seated employees trim bags of recently harvested product. It's like a scene out of Detroit at the height of its automotive might, except rolling off the assembly line here is marijuana. In one corner, there's an Americans with Disabilities Act–compliant bathroom, as well as a fire exit that leads to an alley. A locked side door embedded in an eight-inch-thick wall leads to Avalon's marijuana cultivation area. In the hallway a few feet to the right of this door is the grow room, where ninety plants flower beneath sodium heat lamps. If the carbon monoxide levels in this room exceed two thousand parts per million, horns blare and blue strobe lights turn on as intake and exhaust fans cycle fresh air into the room. From the ceiling of a separate curing room hang a few dozens plants cloned from strains with names such as Avalon White Chunk, Diesel Alien, and Tar Dog.

Everything within the walls of this building materialized in less than ninety days thanks to a wiry, fast-talking, finger-snapping construction contractor who asked to remain anonymous and whose regular work up until now has been mostly high-end residential construction. Indeed, a Newport Beach mansion he built won a seven-page spread in *Better Homes and Gardens*. Valerie Crist, the dispensary's director, is a blonde soccer mom and recently divorced realtor who left the business during the housing bubble and has since invested her life savings in the collective. She says she would have lost everything if it weren't for the contractor, who performed the $500,000 city-required construction at half the cost.

"Our first harvest failed about eight months ago," Crist tells me, explaining that the crop fell victim to spider mites, which infested the plants and rendered them below the dispensary's high-quality standards. "We should have closed our door then, but [he] came and saved us. It was good enough to sell on the street, but we did the right thing. We destroyed it, threw it into trash bags. It was a lot of product for us, probably $40,000 worth of product that we threw away in a couple of days. I cried."

Avalon Wellness sank at least $400,000 into the construction project, money its investors can ill afford to gamble. "We had every city inspector here," the contractor says. "It was a long, tedious process, but we stuck in there and jumped through every hoop. I'm only here because the city of Long Beach opened the front door and said, 'Come on down.'"

The contractor is referring to the Long Beach City Council's vote in March 2010 to enact an ordinance allowing cannabis collectives to operate legally in the city. The law was envisioned as a way to regulate the medical-marijuana dispensaries that were sprouting in buildings throughout the city, moving into storefronts that had been abandoned by failed businesses, sometimes near parks and schools. What Long Beach hoped to accomplish was twofold. On the one hand, the city wanted to make badly needed cash by forcing collectives to spend tens of thousands of dollars or more to apply for permits in accordance with the city's various rules and regulations for growing and distributing marijuana. Secondly, the city wanted to keep those collectives away from schools and parks. By writing the ordinance in such a way, the city would effectively shutter the majority of the clubs that were operating in areas where the city didn't want them, while simultaneously allowing the remainder to compete for permits.

Thus, on September 20, 2010, the city held a lottery to determine which of the several dozen marijuana collectives which had paid the roughly $15,000 upfront application fee would be eligible to receive a permit allowing them to operate in the city. It was a fiasco. The city had spent several thousand dollars on a machine designed to randomly choose Ping-Pong balls stenciled with a combination of numbers and letters, each pertaining to a different collective, but the balls were too big, so officials had to toss them into a recycling bin and hand-select them instead.

Not surprisingly, the carnival-type atmosphere led to immediate claims that the lottery was rigged. According to Assistant City Attorney Michael Mais, Long Beach had successfully used a lottery to allocate flight spots at the tiny Long Beach Airport. "We wanted to limit the number of dispensaries," Mais explained. "We had two choices. We could have a lottery, which I thought was very fair, or we could go with whoever turned their application in first, which I don't think anyone could say was fair."

Predictably, not everybody was happy with the results of the dispensary lottery. "The people who won the lottery thought it was fair, and the people who lost it thought it was unfair," Mais allows. "Other than the fact that the lottery machine failed to work, the lottery was as straight up as any lottery that was ever done. We bent over backward to take any sort of unfairness out of it. We spent a ton of money. It was unfortunate it turned out the way it did, because it was embarrassing."

Like the Long Beach Police Department, which continued to view dispensaries as a source and locus of criminal activity, Mais's boss, City Attorney Robert Shannon, was never a fan of the idea of allowing medical marijuana dispensaries to operate in the city. He insisted that the more than $15,000 in permit fees demanded by Long Beach was justifiable, given the city's dire economic situation and the cost of regulating the dispensaries that his office envisioned.

"We wanted to limit the number of dispensaries, and we wanted to recover our costs," he says. However, Shannon acknowledges, the fee "inadvertently" made it more likely that the "more profit-oriented collectives" would win the lottery. "That was never intended, of course, but that's a fair statement," he says. "It was an unintended consequence." In fact, what started out as a journey into a brave new world where cities could actually benefit from the marijuana industry rapidly backfired into a nightmare where nobody benefited—not the city or its taxpayers, not the cannabis clubs, and least of all, their members, the patients. If anything, what happened in Long Beach arguably sealed the medical-marijuana industry's fate, speeding up the federal government's ongoing effort to drive cannabis back where it has always been: deep into America's underground economy.

— — — — —

I first began unraveling this tale during the trial of the two Joes, at a Long Beach eatery a block from the courthouse where that ridiculous spectacle unfolded, a restaurant called Rock Bottom. As Christopher Glew and I dined on salads and burgers, I mentioned that I'd been hearing rumors about how several of the dispensaries operating in Long Beach were owned by a private investment group led by local businessmen with strong ties to people who worked at city hall.

Glew suggested I talk to Paul Violas, a lawyer whom Glew had met on the courthouse steps several months earlier, as he was leaving a hearing for a client who was going through the city's lottery process. "I had never heard of him before that," he told me. "I think I mentioned I didn't know who he was and he was like, 'Wow, you don't know me?'"

During their chat, Violas made casual reference to a few things about Glew's case, implying, for example, that if it wasn't his—that is, Violas's case—the city didn't consider it important which city prosecutor it appointed. "He called himself a heavy hitter in town," Glew told me. "So I took it as a little bit of braggadocio by him." Violas claimed he was working for a client who already had a building near the courthouse approved for growing medical marijuana. "He said they had this all set up for a grow facility that was going to be utilized in the city and I thought that was interesting. I wanted to know what it was all about, but he didn't really want to provide any more information on it."

Violas had actually pointed in the general direction of the building in question. "It was right over there, behind the courthouse," Glew explained. "At the time, I was kind of curious because I have a whole bunch of clients involved in the lottery process, how do you have a whole place signed off and approved. But he never said to me he was paying anybody off or anything. Obviously that would have resonated with me a little deeper. But the only reason I paid attention to it was first of all, I didn't know the guy at all and it was weird he was approaching me on this case where my clients had been jammed up with the city and he's insinuating he's got some special process."

After talking to Glew, I began interviewing medical-marijuana activists in Long Beach, including several who told me that FBI agents had also interviewed them, although for the most part they refused to provide specifics. "I can't tell you anything about that," said one source. "They did visit me," said another. "Their questions were about public corruption and not the legality of medical marijuana. The statement I gave was that I wasn't aware of any malfeasance and hadn't engaged in any."

By the time I met Violas, I'd already figured out the identity of his big client, the guy who ran the city-approved grow facility that Violas had bragged to Glew about, the local businessman who was rumored to own half a dozen of the collectives that happened to win the city's lottery process. He was John Morris, a silver-haired ex-rugby player in his early sixties, a guy who spoke softly in a vaguely English accent, and with a tendency to end sentences with words such as "babe" and "love" that betrays his Liverpudlian roots.

After emigrating from England, Morris settled in Long Beach in 1972; seven years later, he opened the famed Legends Sports Bar on Second Street in Belmont Shore. In 1988, he pioneered the revival of Pine Street by opening Mum's, an upscale steakhouse and jazz bar, and later Smooth's Sports Grille, which closed in 2010 owing the city $147,000 in unpaid loans. For several years, Morris served as the president of Downtown Long Beach Associates, often clashing with the city over redevelopment, but also charming much of city hall— as well as the newsroom of the *Long Beach Press Telegram* and other local publications. If he was one of the most powerful businessmen in Long Beach, he was also one of the most outspoken, especially against the city's centerpiece redevelopment project of the 1990s, the Pike at Rainbow Harbor.

In 2008, amidst the overall economic downturn that began that year, Morris became eager to explore medical marijuana. He'd recently lost a friend to prostate cancer, and he'd seen how well cannabis had treated the pain. In a recent interview at McKenna's on the Bay, where Morris now works as a manager, he recalled being struck by the thought that he was the perfect guy to implement the city's plan to allow dispensaries to operate in the city as a way to welcome much-needed tax revenue. His pitch to city hall: work with someone you know, rather than open the door to strangers from out of town who might turn out to be shady characters. "How are we going to make this truly work in Long Beach so it's not gang-bangers doing it?" Morris figured. "Let's bring the community into this thing so everyone knows who we are."

I met Morris at the upscale seafood restaurant McKenna's on the Bay, which straddles a waterfront on the westernmost edge of the city, and serves delicious steamed mussels and sushi. Since marijuana collectives aren't allowed to make a profit in California, Morris told me he'd planned to open at least four different storefronts throughout the city, each affiliated with a nearby charity, including Long Beach Memorial Foundation; the city's skate-park program, run by an ex-councilman named Mike Donelon; and the Long Beach Gay and Lesbian Center, whose director, Ron Sylvester, recalls talking to Morris and being excited about the concept.

"I brought it to our board of directors and got back to John and told him that we'd love to be a beneficiary," Sylvester told me. "I kept an eye on what was happening legislatively, and, of course, we're disappointed that it hasn't come to fruition." When he met with city attorney Shannon about the project, Morris brought his lobbyist, Matt Knabe, whose father, Don Knabe, sits on the Los Angeles County Board of Supervisors. Shannon informed Morris that state law prohibited him from opening multiple stores. "The whole concept was odd to me because state law is very clear that you can't make a profit," Shannon recalled.

Morris decided that Shannon had no right to tell him what to do. "As we left that meeting, I said, 'Fuck this,'" Morris recalled. "I've got plenty of friends in town who are believers in this stuff, so I went out and talked to ten or twelve of my buddies." He formed an investment group called SJK—an acronym using his own first initial, plus those belonging to two of his friends and fellow investors, Stu Ledsam and Kurt Schneider. Then Morris set about finding properties throughout the city where SJK could grow and distribute medical marijuana via six supposedly separate collectives.

Because the city required at least three individuals to be on the permit application paperwork for each collective, Morris gathered eighteen people and convinced them to lend their names to the various collectives. He hired a lawyer—Violas—to draw up the articles of corporation and assemble the complex application materials: dozens of pages of personal disclosure forms, rules, regulations and checklists, each requiring the initials of the collective's trio of managing members. To create a nonprofit called the Fourth Street Collective at 1069 Wardlow Road, Morris reached out to Christine Donelon, wife of the former city councilman who ran the skate-park charity Morris hoped to fund. Another was tax accountant Oswaldo Lainez, who handled returns for both Morris and Dee Andrews, a Long Beach councilman. I reached several of the people Morris used to create his network of dispensaries; all of them, including Lainez, professed shock that they had anything to do with the medical-marijuana industry and seemed dismayed that they were being contacted about their involvement.

But without their names, Morris would never have been able to make his plan work, and as the early-summer-2010 filing deadline loomed for collectives that wished to get into the lottery, Morris and Violas summoned the SJK group together for a meeting at Smooth's. Unfortunately, not everyone could make the meeting or otherwise be found in time. So with their permission, Morris forged their signatures on the paperwork. So did his employee, Josh Howard, a onetime marijuana-collective owner who worked for Morris. Howard told me Morris approached him in early 2010 and offered to pay the $15,000 the city required to apply for the upcoming lottery if Howard would help him manage the several collectives Morris was trying to set up. Howard was excited at the opportunity to work with someone who, while clearly tight with the city, seemed to play by his own rules, as if he were untouchable. All the dispensaries were allowed to remain open while they went through the lottery application process, and Howard saw to it that Morris's various clubs did a brisk business. He recalls that Morris would often leave the shops at closing time with thousands of dollars of cash, jumping into the passenger seat of a marked police vehicle.

On the day the lottery applications were due, Morris called Howard. "I need you to start signing signatures," Morris told him. "Half of these people are out of town or I can't get ahold of them. One guy's out of the country." Morris and Howard drove to city hall, scribbling whatever signatures and initials they could find. They parked outside, and Morris went upstairs with a stack of papers that Violas had drawn up while Howard continued to sign names. I obtained all the applications from the city via a California Public Records Act request, and Howard pointed out which signatures he'd forged. The illegible scribbles were easy for him to identify—they looked less like signatures than the wavy lines you see on an EKG—and he pointed out several items that he and Morris completely forgot to initial, which should have guaranteed that the applications would be immediately dismissed as incomplete. In fact, several other non-bogus cannabis collectives had their applications tossed out with no recourse, a move that opened them up to frequent visits from cops and code-enforcement officers, for things as simple as having failed to fill out the application forms correctly.

Morris, who didn't attend the event, recalls receiving text messages each time one of his collectives won the September 20 lottery. To his amazement, he says, five of the six locations he'd lined up had been approved by the city to operate as legitimate marijuana dispensaries. "Everybody fucking thinks we fixed that thing," he told me. "If Shannon had his way, he'd have made sure those balls of ours would never come to the top. . . . The vast majority of management people at city hall, they don't like me, and I don't like them."

Although Morris readily admitted to me that he was involved in no fewer than six different collectives, because his name wasn't listed as a managing member of any of them, he didn't violate the city's ordinance, according to Mais. "To a certain extent, we rely on the honesty of the people we are dealing with," he explained. "As long as their name isn't listed as a management member, we have no way of knowing. You have to assume they are following the rules."

As soon as the city held the lottery, however, it revised its marijuana ordinance. The law already required cannabis clubs to be farther than fifteen hundred feet from a high school and one thousand feet from any kindergarten, elementary, middle, or junior-high school or other dispensary. To these, the city added that no club could be within one thousand feet of a park or beach. Because Long Beach is on the ocean and full of parks, the list of eligible storefronts shrank considerably. Thanks to the new buffer zones, numerous clubs that had won the lottery were now ineligible for a city permit after all, including one operated by Morris. Meanwhile, however, the city kept adding new construction prerequisites—fire alarms, security systems, and carbon monoxide monitoring systems—to further whittle down the field.

In what amounted to a bait-and-switch maneuver, the city had to set up a refund-application process to collectives that had won the lottery but were subsequently zoned out of contention. Ultimately, of the five locations tied to Morris that won the lottery, just two ever opened their doors—both of them at addresses previously occupied by Byron and Grumbine's two Long Beach collectives. Of those, only one continues to operate, but Morris and his investors had to back out of the business because they ran out of money. "We never made a fucking dollar," he said. "My SJK guys, of the $500,000 they outlaid, I don't think they'll get any of that back."

Morris eventually fired Howard and a woman named Nichole West, who says she drew up a business plan for SJK. West, a bright young woman and true believer in the medical-marijuana cause, had spoken at city council meetings, urging the city to implement a sensible medical-marijuana ordinance. She'd also used her real estate skills to find locations for clubs, including those operated by Morris, to locate, but she claims Morris never paid her and owes her thousands of dollars, a claim echoed by Howard, who complained to one of SJK's investors, a famous soccer player who seemed sympathetic.

After he did so, one of Morris's lawyers sent him a letter threatening to sue him and referring to his allegations as "untrue" and "grossly slanderous."

– – – – –

If Morris and other collective operators who managed to win the lottery were upset at the city, so were those whose Ping-Pong balls weren't chosen, or who refused to pay or could not afford the $15,000 fee to play the game in the first place.

Larry Parks, who owned the 1 A.M. collective, first became suspicious about the city's program weeks earlier, when he paid a $2,000 consulting fee to Morris's attorney, Violas. "I wanted to get his thoughts about the lottery process and what he thought my chances were," Parks recalls. "He wanted me to hire him for $2,000 a month and told me his clients don't get bothered by the city. He called it 'good lawyering,' and said he'd need $5,000 here and $5,000 there to spread around."

Violas claimed to be "good friends" with Erik Sund, Long Beach's business-relations manager and director of the city's medical-marijuana program. "Mr. Violas told me that if I paid him money, he would be able to guarantee acceptance of my patient-cooperative group's application for a Long Beach city permit," Parks later stated in a sworn deposition. "When I asked him how he could do this, he told me . . . my group might have to make monetary contributions to city projects or to city officials." Parks declined to take on Violas as a lawyer. Another dispensary operator told me Violas solicited a $2,000 bribe, which he said would guarantee that the dispensary would be able to operate legally in Long Beach, although the source said he didn't know if Violas ever bribed anyone with the cash or simply pocketed it himself.

I asked Violas about these allegations and, in particular, his conversation with Parks during an interview at his office in downtown Long Beach. He arrived fifteen minutes late, offering me a harsh handshake and a tight smile. He told me that while he maintains "cordial" relationships with Sund and other city officials, he has never made any such guarantees. "I categorically deny that I've ever promised any client that payment of money to a city official will result in favorable treatment," he insisted.

Violas didn't deny that he'd helped Morris draw up paperwork for his various collectives, and claimed there was nothing illegal about creating a for-profit business partnership for the purpose of investing in and subleasing property to various medical-marijuana dispensaries. Such denials aside, Violas claimed Morris ripped him off. "I will say this," he told me. "I have yet to take a client to small claims court. I don't think it's appropriate. I think at the end of the day if I take on a client that doesn't honor his obligations to me, then I made a mistake in choosing a client."

Morris's former landlord, a local restaurateur in Long Beach who asked not to be identified by name, complained that Morris also left her in the lurch. The owner of numerous commercial properties throughout the city, including two she rented to Byron and Grumbine until they were raided and put out of business by the city, she actually testified in their defense, unsuccessfully trying to assure the jury that it was her handyman who was responsible for the bad wiring that led to Byron being charged with electricity theft. After the two Joes had been busted and were unable to pay her rent, she told me, Morris approached her looking to rent the two buildings, and several others. She signed the paperwork renting several locations to SJK, which in turn sublet to the various "independent" dispensaries. One of the locations had been approved to be a grow house after the city added a requirement to its pot ordinance requiring all marijuana collectives to cultivate their own product.

Her relationship with Morris took a nosedive when an entire crop failed after the power went out at the building, thus turning off thousands of dollars worth of growing equipment. "They abandoned the properties and I never heard from them again," the landlord complained. "I got this message from them saying it is not in your best interest to talk to anyone about this." She added that she wasn't surprised Morris and SJK came out big in the lottery. "I have no proof," she told me, "but I suspect the lottery was a fake. How else can you explain all of those locations winning?"

— — — —

Unlike Morris, who had friendly enough ties with some people at city hall, but more important, deep enough pockets to raise the cash to spin the lottery wheel, most of the dispensary operators in Long Beach didn't have the money or the motivation to pay the cash. Lawyer Matt Pappas now represents Parks and several other collective operators whom the city fined, raided, or both for violating its medical-marijuana ordinance.

Pappas is convinced the city's entire pot policy is corrupt to the core, and moreover, he believes that Long Beach officials are out to get him, something he says is evidenced by the fact that the city refused to grant him a business license, and even threatened to have him arrested for practicing in the city without one. "I don't know what's happening . . . but there's something wrong," Pappas told me in an interview at his office, an abandoned pot dispensary that one of his clients was letting him use. "When people say they can engineer things and you won't get raided since you're paying money that gets spread about, it's awfully suspect. Think about it: the city is taking money from some collectives and not issuing them citations and going out and raiding the ones that aren't paying the money."

One of Pappas's clients, Mike Genara, applied for the lottery, but soon after, the city began sending code-enforcement officers to his collective, threatening his landlord, and issuing him up to $50,000 in fines over a period of several months. The police also showed up and filed misdemeanor charges—violating the city's marijuana ordinance—against his security guard and manager. "They used every kind of tactic that you can imagine," Genara told me. "It was just so overwhelming."

Until she voluntarily closed the dispensary late last year, another one of Pappas's clients, Katherine Aldrich, operated 562 Collective in the north Long Beach neighborhood of Bixby Knolls. She also refused to pay the city's permit fee and didn't participate in the lottery. On February 15, 2011, the police raided her collective while she was taking her daughter to the orthodontist. Security footage filmed during the raid shows plainclothes officers, accompanied by Sund, standing in her lobby. No arrests were made, but Aldrich received a fine. The cops returned again three months later, again without a warrant. When her employees refused to open the safe, police arrested them but left empty-handed. Sund was present for that raid, too. "He's a business-license approver," Aldrich argued. "Why he's out there participating in these raids, I have no idea."

As it turned out, the cops were using an informant against the collectives. A day before police raided Aldrich's collective, the shop had received a visit from a young African American man named Emmanuel Walker, who'd carried a written doctor's recommendation for cannabis. Aldrich didn't discover Walker's visit until after she received a call from Dallas Alexander, operator of another club, Dank City. Like Aldrich, Alexander had paid only a token fee of $500 to the city, instead of the $15,000. "I was summarily rejected," he said. Not long thereafter, on March 17, 2011, the police raided his shop. That morning, Alexander was pulling up at the dispensary when he saw squad cars. He walked next door to a tire shop, whose owners told him they'd seen someone get out of a police van and enter the collective, then get back in the vehicle just moments before the raid began. They'd captured the event on their shop's security camera, the tape of which they showed to Alexander.

A few hours later, after the police left with a haul of confiscated cannabis and three employees in handcuffs, Alexander checked the paperwork of the last patient who gained entry and came up with a photocopy of Walker's doctor's note, which helpfully included his signature and an image of his California driver's license. It was the same person Alexander had just seen getting into the cop car in the security footage. "He'd just come in and bought a gram of King Louie the XVIII, one of our most popular strains," Alexander told me. "That's when I called everyone and said, 'Do not let this guy in; he's the snitch.'"

On March 31, 2011, Walker visited the now-shuttered Canna Collective Long Beach (CCLB). After hearing from Alexander, Josh Howard, who worked at CCLB at the time, hung on the lobby wall a photocopy of Walker's doctor's note, along with R.C.I.: DO NOT LET IN! in bold black marker (the acronym stands for "reliable confidential informant"). Unfortunately, CCLB's employees failed to heed the warning. "The girls weren't paying attention," he says. "A few days later, they just let the guy in, and that was the day CCLB got raided." Howard checked the paperwork to see if Walker had stopped by on the day of the raid. "I go look through the files," he recalls, "and yep, that's him."

Walker's next stop was the Giving Tree collective on Broadway Avenue, just east of downtown Long Beach. But he chose a week when the dispensary's computer system for verifying new patients wasn't working. Mark Rosebush, one of the shop's owners, who had already been alerted to watch out for informants, was on duty when Walker knocked on the door. "I had a sign up saying we can't verify new patients, but he came back a second day and a third time," Rosebush says. "Finally, on the last time I refused him, he was insistent as hell." Rosebush wondered why. "There were a million weed stores in the city—it's like getting a six-pack from 7-Eleven—so why does he want to come to my store so bad?"

The more Rosebush refused to sell marijuana to Walker, the more insistent Walker grew, so much so that Rosebush got the distinct feeling the conversation was being recorded. He began yelling at Walker. "You are nothing but an RCI, a fucking rat-bastard snitch," he screamed. "And I am putting your picture up here and sending it everywhere else. You are behind all this. Get your goddamn ass out of here!" When Rosebush followed Walker out of the building, he saw several men he knew to be cops walking toward the store. Walker made a "cut" sign by running his finger along his throat. The officers stopped in their tracks. "I lifted my hands in the air—like, 'I know who you are'—and walked back down the alley."

It's unclear how long Walker's career as a snitch might have continued, but in any case it ended just a few months later, when paramedics arrived at the 600 block of Cerritos Avenue at about 7:00 in the morning on May 17, 2011. They were responding to a call about a man who had been stabbed in an alley north of downtown, just a block from Long Beach's Franklin Middle School and the Museum of Latin American Art. An ambulance raced the victim, a thirty-two-year-old man named Stephen Brown, to the hospital in critical condition, but he died of his injuries at 5:00 that evening. Meanwhile, police began an investigation that quickly led them to two suspects: the snitch, Walker—who was arrested the day Brown died—and an accomplice named Norvin Dizadre, thirty-three, who was arrested on May 19. Both men were booked for murder, robbery, and kidnapping.

According to the initial press release on the crime issued by the Long Beach Police Department, Brown was an acquaintance of both Walker and Dizadre and "had been at a social event" with his attackers "prior to the assault, which occurred as a result of a dispute," the nature of which wasn't specified. However, police believed Walker and Dizadre had attacked Brown at a house "before dragging him away from the house to conceal their involvement."

Speaking of concealing involvement, though, at the bottom of the press release about the murder, police invited anyone with information about the assault or the suspects to contact homicide investigators. The statement didn't mention that police had been working with Walker to harass cannabis collectives that weren't on the city's list of approved dispensaries. After a brief trial that received no headlines in the local press, both Walker and Dizadre were convicted of second-degree murder and sentenced to fifteen years to life in prison.

– – – – –

Perhaps the ultimate irony in Long Beach's ill-fated foray into the medical-marijuana business is that even the select group of collectives that did win the lottery and that haven't been subjected to heavy fines or raids by the city still had no guarantee they won't be shut down. This elite group of collectives, which includes Avalon Wellness Collective, numbers roughly a dozen and has formed a group called Long Beach Collective Association (LBCA). The group's lawyers include both Violas and Rick Brizendine, whose name turned up in a search-warrant affidavit filed by the Orange County Sheriff's Department when it raided Belmont Shore Natural Care Collective on November 8, 2011.

According to sheriff's officials, the department raided the collective after finding ties between Belmont Shore Natural Care and several Orange County collectives run by a silent investor who, they assert, was using Brizendine to launder his money. Brizendine returned an initial telephone call seeking an interview, but he subsequently failed to answer his phone. But according to the sheriff's warrant, Brizendine's client was a mysterious silent investor named John Walker, who owned several other dispensaries in Orange County, which the ever-present Violas had helped him launch. When deputies raided Belmont Shore Natural Care, they also raided several Orange County dispensaries allegedly owned by Walker, discovering evidence of black-market marijuana sales, as well as piles of cash and firearms, including AK-47 assault rifles.

While Long Beach's incoherent medical-marijuana policy may have been intended to take cannabis out of the hands of black-market and organized-crime players, it may have had the opposite effect. Just ask Larry King—not the retired television talk show host, but an honest businessman who saw an opportunity to get involved in medical marijuana in Long Beach and lost everything in the process. King literally went broke trying to put together a dispensary that never opened its doors or provided cannabis to a single patient, and the only consolation for him was that, unlike all the other dispensary operators who were screwed over in the city's lottery process, he finally got his application fee refunded. A long-time retail-store entrepreneur in the city, King entered the medical-marijuana trade in 2010, the same year his mother died from lung cancer, a years-long battle that he helped her fight with vaporized marijuana instead of pills whose side effects twice sent her to the emergency room.

"Long Beach at the time was known as the Wild West," King recalls. "There were seventy or eighty dispensaries operating there, and the police were known to do nothing." When the city passed its ordinance allowing cannabis collectives to register for a lottery, King was exhilarated. "I thought it was great they were going to take this industry away from the gangbangers and tattoo-wearing cartel guys—and not only allow us to grow the medicine ourselves, but require us to do so," he says.

To comply with the city's elaborate code requirements for his facility, King says, he sank $220,000 into construction bills and permits. But when the city added proximity to parks to its list of restrictions, King suddenly found himself zoned out of contention. Adding insult to injury was the fact that Violas bragged to him that he had clients who were being allowed to relocate, an option that wasn't available to him. Violas offered to fix things for King, but required an upfront fee of $4,000, King says, just to place him on the client list.

King never opened his dispensary and now faces the loss of his own house, which he had to mortgage to pay his debts. He blames feckless city officials for changing their tune about marijuana midstream. In particular, he blames his local councilwoman, Gerrie Schipske, who at one public meeting waved a piece of paper in the air in a gesture reminiscent of Joe McCarthy and his famous blacklist of card-carrying communists. The paper was a recent article in the *Long Beach Press Telegram* about how the police had made a large seizure of marijuana at the Long Beach Airport, a haul that had been smuggled to the city by the Russian mafia. The police claimed that the pot was being supplied to local dispensaries.

Coincidentally, King, who happens to be of Russian-Jewish extraction, says that he did in fact get a visit from the Russian mob just after Schipske's speech, when the city changed its rules and disqualified him from the lottery. Apparently the mob sensed a good opportunity to move in and win a share of the marijuana marketplace now that legitimate players were dropping out of the game. Two men who wore flashy chains and garish tracksuits and spoke in heavy eastern European accents walked into his defunct dispensary one afternoon and made him an offer they thought he'd be a fool to refuse.

"We can fix this," the Russians told him. "We have you run this business, and we'll handle the city. You don't have to worry about that anymore."

King politely declined their offer. "Are you guys Russian Mafia?" he asked.

He was joking, but an uncomfortable silence filled the room.

"They didn't answer my question," King says. "They just sort of smiled at me."

7 | The Green Spot

"That's some pretty good-looking herb you got there."

It's about 10:00 AM on a brisk November day, and I'm driving my rental car out of Oakland International Airport. Christopher Glew is talking to his client, a man who for the purposes of this book we'll call Lucky, who has just opened up his carry-on backpack to reveal three ounces of freshly manicured marijuana. The weed amounts to a sample kit of a freshly harvested Snowcap strain which Lucky grew at one of his nurseries in Southern California. He plans to show it to a potential buyer in the Bay Area, in the hopes of arranging a large-scale deal—although Glew knows nothing of this plan and Lucky won't reveal it to me until later, when he apparently figures that I might somehow help him pull it off.

At the moment, we're heading to a meeting with the owners of a medical-marijuana delivery service called the Green Spot, the largest such operation in the San Francisco Bay Area. Instead of his usual pinstripe-suit-and-monogrammed-cufflinks courtroom

121

attire, Glew is dressed in jeans and a black-and-orange leather jacket with the Harley Davidson logo splashed across the shoulders. Lucky is wearing a Los Angeles Angels of Anaheim baseball cap, a baggy designer jersey, and even baggier black jeans. He's in a particularly good mood, and hasn't stopped talking since he got in the car.

"You know what's interesting?" Lucky asks.

As usual, he doesn't wait for an answer.

"I called TSA to find out how much I could take on the plane and they said it's all determined by the doctor."

"TSA said that, really?" Glew asks, not buying it.

"Yeah," Lucky says. "And then I called Southwest Airlines and they said, 'We have no policy at all about weed.' So I've been flying with three or four ounces now. The last time I flew, I took it right out on my seat tray and started looking through the samples."

"No you didn't," Glew says.

"I swear to God, I did," Lucky insists. "I'll do it on the way back. I'll film the whole thing. I should put it on YouTube, because everyone I've told about this can't believe I would do it. But I had to bring some samples on the plane because I've got some stuff that will get some amazing [prices] up here."

The high-grade marijuana Lucky is carrying sells for $800 a pound in California, but could easily earn $2,000 or $2,500 per pound in New York City. Or at least that's what Lucky says. He would know because, as it happens, he arranges cross-country deals every few weeks. "You sell in the right place, and there you go, you're making $1,300 a pound. Do a hundred deals like that, and well, that's what everyone is trying to do out here: pack up as many of these things as they can and ship them back east."

As we head north from the industrial outskirts of Oakland into the steep, tree-lined hills of Berkeley, Lucky's lecture about the economics of pot smuggling rapidly devolves into a litany against the Mexican drug cartels he says are ruining the industry. "They come up here and buy strains from Americans—we're talking California growers who have high-end strains," he says. "And they'll buy these clones that are guaranteed female. They buy the plants! They've learned enough now to turn some of these plants into mothers, so they are learning to clone. And that is something they've never done in the past—you've never seen the Mexicans cloning."

Lucky and other California-based pot cultivators and distributors have no choice but to grow their crops on their own land, or on rented properties, like warehouses, where they can hide large indoor nurseries. The cartels, meanwhile, tend to establish vast outdoor plantations deep inside US National Forest areas. "They're camping out there and have so much time on their hands while their gardens are developing, so they start making speed," Lucky complains. "They're making amphetamines because they can turn that around in a week and use those revenues to generate and finance their gardens."

As the cartels have become more adept at competing with their American competitors, they're constantly on the hunt for access to not only new, higher-end strains, but also technical expertise. "I was personally offered a large sum of money to go to Michoacan and teach them how to make oils and extracts," he says, referring to the various concentrated byproducts of marijuana, mostly liquids like hash oil that pack a powerful high, or solids that can be turned into pill form or baked into edible products like pot brownies. These products can be made purely from the "trim," or excess leaves that are typically manicured off the marijuana before sale, and which usually end up as garden waste.

"Let's say you have a million-dollar garden," Lucky explains. "The trim is 15 percent of your yield. The Mexicans want to learn how to use it so they can add another $150,000 to [their] revenues. So these guys have realized they have a lot of trim and now they're paying people to come down and teach them—offering to put people up in nice, beautiful million-dollar homes that overlook the ocean, and all the women that you want, and someone offered me . . . that a couple of weeks ago."

Lucky says he refused the offer because he didn't have the "political ties" to feel safe while south of the border. "I would never go to Mexico," he says. "But they're looking for people and they're willing to pay big money. I can guarantee you: in my little circle of people that I've taught how to make the crap, there's somebody that's hungry enough for twenty or thirty grand right now that will jump on that bandwagon. It's just going to be a matter of who that guy is. And once he's done that, they're going to learn that trade, and then it just becomes infectious, and now watch what they're smuggling in: oils and hash and pot that sells in America for $1,500 a pound and they've got it for $600 a pound!"

So far, there's no evidence that the cartels are smuggling oils, extracts, or edibles into the United States, but Lucky's right about their growing sophistication when it comes to breaking into the high-grade medical-marijuana market. On November 15, 2011, for example, US Department of Homeland Security agents seized seventeen tons of marijuana on the US-Mexico border when they discovered a tunnel that appears to be the passage of one of the largest cross-border smuggling operations in recent years. According to an Associated Press story on the bust, the tunnel was some four hundred yards long and stretched between a pair of warehouses on either side of the border—one in San Diego and the other in Tijuana. The feds told the AP that the tunnel was "one of the most significant secret passages ever found on the US-Mexico border."

Both US and Mexican feds cooperated on the bust. Nine tons were retrieved from the warehouse in San Diego and eight tons were found on the Mexican side of the border. Agents apparently had the US warehouse under surveillance, and followed two men "in a truck packed with about three tons of pot." A California Highway

Patrol officer pulled the truck over and "was overwhelmed by the smell," the AP reported.

Of course there's nothing too unusual about the feds seizing tons of pot headed into the US from south of the border. Two similar tunnels discovered in 2010, for example, led to the seizure of some fifty tons of weed. But what made this particular bust interesting is the *kind* of marijuana that was seized. It wasn't the generic Mexican brick weed, but stuff that wouldn't have looked out of place on the shelves of the most well-appointed dispensaries in California. To top it off, the Mexican pot was even packaged to look like homegrown medical marijuana, complete with labels that had the names of all-American-sounding strains such as Sprite, Bud Light, and Captain America.

– – – – –

Green Spot Delivery is the Bay Area's largest medical-marijuana delivery service.

The business office is a converted Victorian-era house located on a leafy block and next door to a breakfast diner. Hoyt, one of the company's owners, is tall and blond, and his square jaw, steady gaze, and lanky good looks suggest the confidence of a college-educated jock. He sends his secretary out on a coffee run while he explains how, just a few months earlier—the office is so new that you can still smell the white paint drying on the interior walls—he opened the Green Spot with his silent-investor associate, a man who for the purposes of this book prefers to be identified as El Machino.

His interest in medical marijuana started in 2006, when he severed his middle finger while opening a bottle of wine at a Los Angeles restaurant where he was working as a bartender. Doctors prescribed Hoyt a regimen of painkillers, but he didn't like the side effects: drowsiness and itchy skin. His neighbor, an older woman who smoked pot to treat her chronic migraines, suggested he try out Kushmart, a marijuana dispensary on Hollywood Boulevard. "I tried some indica, which she said was good for pain, and it worked," he recalls. "I still feel pain in my forearm and bicep, but now I can relieve the pain when I need to."

At the time, both L.A. and San Francisco were being over-run with storefront dispensaries, Hoyt figured, and most of them weren't the kinds of places where he or his upscale, business execu-tive-type friends really felt comfortable. Why not create a company that would deliver marijuana to customers in the privacy of their own home, customers who lived in communities that had either outlawed or driven away storefront locations? Ultimately, he settled on Berkeley because it offered convenient access to a host of East Bay cities that had no dispensaries: Walnut Creek, Pleasant Hill, Concord, Danville, Pleasanton, Dublin, Livermore, Oakley, Brent-wood, and Martinez.

"Actually, Concord has one or two [dispensaries], but they are operating illegally," Hoyt adds. "From what I hear, they're paying a $1,000 fine a day, and you have to walk in [through] a back alley."

"That one is shady," Glew agrees. "They are going to be shut down."

On our drive into town just minutes earlier, we'd passed by rows of large warehouses on either side of the freeway. According to Lucky, several of them were recently set up to house illegal dis-pensaries. "Right now is time for 'turn and burns,'" Lucky explains. "Everybody that's growing is just coming down the mountain, rent-ing a place for two months, and they're going to blast off ads for twenty-five dollars an eighth, and instead of selling them to a collec-tive, they're going to retail their pounds."

In other words, instead of selling their weed for $1,000 to $3,000 per pound to a dispensary, these outfits will come up with online and even print advertisements in local alternative newspapers, advertising themselves as legitimate cannabis collectives and dealing directly to consumers, one ounce or eighth-ounce at a time. Doing so drives their per-pound rate up to $5,000 or so, and since you can rent a warehouse for $5,000 to $10,000 per month, Lucky figures, it only takes a few pounds to pay off a landlord and by, say, a month later, when the cops finally figure out what you're up to, you've already sold your crop and are now a few hundred thousand dollars richer.

"There are collectives and then there are 'collectives,'" Glew interjects. "There are the ones that are actually saying, 'Let's go get a lawyer, try to be a mainstay in the community, try to be legit. And then there are the guys like Lucky just described." A year or so ago, before court rulings tightened the rules, he adds, anybody could start their own collective by simply designating themselves as "compassionate caregivers" for their dozens or hundreds or thousands of customers. All they needed was a so-called "caregiver certificate" signed by both parties.

"So now you've got one guy with a club and ten thousand customers, and the courts didn't like that," says Glew. "They started coming up with all these rules: a caregiver has to be in the same county, then they limited it more: it has to be a relative or friend, not just someone you're selling weed to; you gotta be mowing their lawn or picking them up from doctor's appointments." When the courts finally ruled that caregivers have to prove they have preexisting familial relationships with the marijuana patient, the medical-marijuana industry simply dropped the pretense and sought legal protection for collectives under a California supreme court ruling, the so-called *Mensch* decision, that allowed patients to collectively and cooperatively grow and distribute marijuana.

Thanks to that ruling, any California resident with a doctor's note can legally obtain a "reasonable" amount of marijuana—what's reasonable is determined by their physician—from their nearest marijuana dispensary, rather than having to grow it on their own or obtain it from a mythical family caregiver. But what about people who live in cities without dispensaries? "There was definitely a need out there," Hoyt continues. "All these patients were driving all the way out here, through the tunnel to Oakland, to Harborside. A lot of our clients are people who don't want to go to a collective, or have some stoner in an AC/DC shirt smelling like smoke come up to their house."

Instead, Green Spot delivery drivers wear the informally preppy attire you'd associate with an express, door-to-door delivery service—a dark polo shirt, khaki slacks or shorts, and a baseball cap. The marijuana is placed in an airtight plastic canister with the Green Spot logo and what Hoyt refers to as "Prop. 215 verbiage," which explains that this is medical weed, not that other kind you buy on the streets. There's also a clear window so patients can see the medicine once they pull the canister from the unmarked manila folder that the driver hands them.

"Everyone up here wants to see the medicine," Hoyt explains. "Apparently in Southern California they don't care—that's just what I heard." The driver is equipped with an iPhone that can plug into a credit-card reader so that they don't have to worry about carrying cash. "The receipt is mailed to them if they like; if they don't, it's not," he says. "So on your bill, it just comes up Green Spot Delivery. That's it. In and out."

This is all old news to Lucky, who used to run his own delivery service in Southern California, before he sold it to a wealthy Republican businessman. "I used to do the delivery thing," he boasts, "but I transitioned out of it." Sounding as if he's just finished reading a Malcolm Gladwell book for aspiring capitalists, Lucky begins lecturing Hoyt about how the marijuana industry's "front-liners" (that is, the people who will come to dominate the business once legalization occurs) must possess the "forward-thinking capacity" to constantly stay "on the cutting edge" of the pot trade.

"I truly believe that today, it's all about branding," Lucky declares, his raspy voice rising as he grows increasingly excited. "In five or ten years from now—if we put our balls to the wall today—we can be the Jack Daniels of tomorrow, the Johnnie Walker Reds, the Jim Beams of the future—all those guys put their balls on the line. Back in the day, Jack Daniels became Jack Daniels because he kept his balls on the line."

"He was a moonshiner during Prohibition," Glew observes.

"That's what I'm getting at," Lucky enthuses. "It's true! We don't see it because we're in the eye of the fucking storm right now. But in twenty or thirty years we'll look back and go, 'Wow, we were right in the middle of it!'"

According to Hoyt, the Green Spot's success going forward won't only rely on dependable customer service and quality of product. "We see the future of this industry in packaging," he says. "For a long time, it's been run like a farmers' market. You go, you look at the product, weigh it out, and put it in a bag. Who's going to remember that? It's a guy with a hat at the farmers' market and you like his carrots. But if he or she has a name and packaging, you're going to remember it and order it again. It's the consistency of product and medicine that a patient wants to have, and it's the packaging they remember."

Green Spot's next venture, he adds, will be to grow and deliver clone plants to customers. Currently, they refer clients who want to grow their own weed to Harborside, which specializes in clones. The challenge, he explains, is figuring out how to discreetly deliver actual plants as opposed to small packages of marijuana. "Right now, I just want to focus on getting the right audience—get the right market of people that really want the delivery," Hoyt says. "We carry only high-grade medicine—two outdoors and five indoors. We have a variation of hybrids of indicas and sativas. We state on our website the medical benefits of each one."

Lucky can barely contain himself. "You know what would be really good PR for you?" he asks. "Send a group of patients out and say, 'One of the things we do at Green Spot is take pride in the life-style of our patients. We went out to Mr. Jones and saw the lights he was using and he wasting all this energy, so we put these kind of lights in.' Do the three or four simple things you can do to someone's house to make it green, so now you've got magazines that want to do stories on you because you're making a greener environment for your patients. That term 'green' is so fucking hot right now. The Green Spot can be a healthy spot to go paperless, LED lights, all that stuff—really capture those dollars that are coming in from those green efforts. There are a lot of people out there trying to inject dollars into that green movement. And all of a sudden the Green Spot is saying, 'We went to our patient in Rossmoor or Willow Creek, and we changed their toilet and plumbing! We did this, we did that!'"

"He's not actually on meth," Glew jokes, glancing around the table. "He's on coffee."

"It's the mocha," Hoyt says, laughing. "What'd you put in the mocha?"

Several minutes—and several of Lucky's stream-of-consciousness-style revelations about the marijuana business—later, El Machino arrives, his presence announced by the roar of his approaching Harley Davidson 127" Road King. Hoyt's silent partner in the Green Spot is a muscular, middle-aged man with a goatee and a wide grin, who in his other life owns a small mortgage company that despite California's plummeting real estate market regularly pulls down six or seven figures in profits each year. With the Green Spot, El Machino's not just a partner, he's also a patient, so to speak. Before Hoyt approves any edible for delivery, like those provided by Berkeley-based Yak Edibles, he first tests it on El Machino.

"Yak Edibles says you just need one dose, one capsule, to get high," Hoyt says. "So I ask El Machino if he's tried the capsule and he goes, 'Oh yeah, I tried five—five at once. It felt great. It solved all my problems. Which ones? I don't know.' But we know that if five of these are working for El Machino, one of them will be just fine for one of our normal patients."

"He's kind of like chupacabra," Lucky jokes. "Does he really exist? We don't know. But he might eat anything!"

Besides Yak Edibles, the Green Spot has also partnered with a company called Medi-Cone, which according to Hoyt was founded by a friend of his who was a student at Richard Lee's Oaksterdam University. Medi-Cone makes extra-large, cone-sized joints that contain a mixture of medium-grade marijuana buds and kief. Each joint is made from paper formed in Amsterdam and then sent back to California, where it is filled with marijuana and packaged in a plastic tube with a top that easily pops off and on, allowing you to keep the roach from stinking up your car or house when you're done smoking it.

The cones are one of the Green Spot's most popular delivery orders. "Basically we've co-branded with an established entity and we have great feedback already," El Machino says. "And we did the same thing with Yak. That's just a business-model kind of thing: find somebody who's established and try to partner with them. Medi-Cone has some of the best joints out there for sure."

Clearly El Machino is a fan. Do we have any Medi-Cones here?" he asks.

"Actually no, I blew it," Hoyt admits, before suddenly breaking into a grin.

"What are we talking about?" he says, laughing. "I run a delivery service: I can have it delivered out here in 10 minutes. Let's place an order. We can have it delivered to your place."

— — — — —

On the way to El Machino's house in a suburban Alameda County town not far from Berkeley, Lucky is waxing nostalgic.

Although he's lived the past two decades in Southern California, he grew up in the Bay Area, and this is his home turf. As we pass underneath a bridge, he points to an off-ramp and begins laughing hysterically. Apparently, we've just passed the scene of one of the most haphazardly dangerous acts of his manifestly reckless life, which occurred about twenty years ago, just before noon one Christmas Day in the 1980s, when Lucky was twenty-five-years old and on the way from his apartment in Walnut Creek to meet his family in Berkeley.

That day, he was driving his brand-new BMW 325, which he'd recently loaned to a friend of his who'd needed it for a late-night fast-food run. Unfortunately, although not surprisingly, his friend was stoned, and on the way into the drive-through lane of the Jack in the Box, he clipped the yellow pole, denting the side of the car. Lucky had been steaming about that dent for two weeks. As he exited the freeway heading the opposite direction we are now, he pulled alongside a cream-colored Ford Maverick. The two men in the car nodded in admiration at his BMW as they both sped through the Caldicott Tunnel.

As he exited the tunnel he sped past the Maverick, right into the path of a blue Chevy Corsica driven by a man and woman who, judging by their dress, were also headed to a family holiday gathering, and who were trying to get over in the right-hand lane to make their exit. Lucky could see that the man had no intention of slowing down, even though it looked like his wife was pleading with him to let Lucky pass in front of them. "It's a fun turn, especially in BMW," Lucky explains. "I'm looking at the guy like, 'Are you fucking kidding me? Are you really going to do this?'" The man maintained eye contact with Lucky as their two lanes merged into the freeway exit.

"Fuck it," Lucky figured. "I've got this huge dent in my door. I'm just going to ram this guy."

Steering slightly to the left, Lucky sideswiped the Corsica, whose rearview mirror shot up into the sky. Edging in front of the other car, he saw the wife yelling at the husband. Lucky stepped on the gas and didn't slow down until he reached his friend's house, so he could hide his car in the garage. Then he called 911 and made up a ridiculous tale: he was getting off the freeway and tried to wave a friendly "Merry Christmas" greeting to two guys in a cream-colored Maverick, one of whom promptly pointed a gun at his face, scaring him so badly that he tried to race away, at which point some guy and his wife in a Corsica tried to run him off the freeway. "These people are going to call you," he told the dispatcher. "You have to give them my number so I can explain what happened." Sure enough, less than an hour later, the husband, who had also called 911, telephoned to apologize to Lucky, who still laughs at his absurd behavior, which, among other things, hadn't even come to close to totaling his BMW.

At El Machino's house, a Suzuki-motorcycle-driving Green Spot delivery man drops off four grams of Lavender Kush, Purple Kush, Blue Dream Indoor, and Grape Ape, plus a couple of Medi-Cones and a few Yak Edibles, totaling exactly $302. Dressed in khaki slacks and a black polo shirt, the driver shows how his iPhone is set up with a PayNet app and a card reader that plugs into his earphone jack, thus allowing him to record the transaction in just a few seconds. "I just type in your account number, you swipe the card, the amount gets sent to you in an e-mail," he says. "You sign, your signature is saved, and you get the delivery, and in the package there's a lighter and a business card."

"Pretty slick, huh?" El Machino says as the Suzuki speeds off. "This is what I am able to bring to the table: a corporate structure. I'm not a corporate-type guy, but it's good to have the structure—and

be cool—in this business. That's what I'm all about: having a struc-
turally applied model and [being] super fucking cool about it. We
want to be around cool people, because we're fun and we're cool,
we get it done and we have the best stuff and good service. We want
clients like me: I have money, I know what I want, and I don't want
any hassles or bullshit."

Lucky is busily sampling the freshly delivered weed. He unwraps
a Medi-Cone and takes a few deep puffs before passing it around.
When the large joint comes back his way, he marvels at the color of
the ash on the tip. "This is a gorgeous fucking thing," he declares.
"When you see ash that's real white, it's ash that doesn't have a lot
of chemicals in the weed. It's flushed out real clean. A lot of the time
when you see black in the ash, it's from the weed." He takes another
drag. "This is an Urkle," he announces, referring to Purple Urkle, an
indica strain popular among cannabis connoisseurs for its lavender
color, mellow taste, and lazy, insomnia-combating body high.

"Yeah," says El Machino. "What's cool is this guy doesn't use
shake for these things—he actually uses the bottom buds. You can
taste the quality."

"This guy's a pro," Lucky concurs. "But you can tell this is old."

Lucky examines the wrapping for the joint and points out that
there's no date anywhere that documents when the joint was prepared. "There's no born-on date, dude," he says. "All of these should
have born-on dates. When was it rolled? You guys should do those,
and if it's been sitting on a shelf for more than two weeks, we're
done with it. We're not going to deal some stale-ass weed. Who
wants to smoke a joint that's been sitting on a shelf for two fucking
years?"

Lucky may be high as a bird right now, and talking faster than
a jackrabbit jumps, but he knows the business, and El Machino is
nodding his head enthusiastically, taking note. "That is what I like
about the position that we're in," he says, puffing on the joint. "We

can go back to them with that [criterion] and start doing that, and when we start printing our own labels we can do that, too. It's all about branding, service, and quality control."

Quality control? Did someone say quality control? There's an app for that, says Lucky. "Have you seen the fucking growbots?" he asks, eyes wide with excitement. "You put one in your garden and it goes through and can recognize how far your plants are from each other and it sticks a sensor into the soil of each plant and reads the PPMs and PHs—"

"Shut the fuck up!" El Machino interrupts. He leans forward, blowing smoke and passing the joint around the table.

"Absolutely," Lucky says, not stopping. "Whatever the plant needs, it will get. And you can control it from your phone. So you can be in Costa Rica and check into your garden on your app, and see that this plant, the leaves are curling, or whatever."

"That would have been great for the pods," El Machino says, referring to the original business idea he and Hoyt had considered several months ago, before opting for a delivery service instead. The pod idea had to do with Proposition 19, which would have allowed California adults to each grow twenty-five square feet of cannabis.

"I have land where there are warehouses, and what I originally wanted to do was set up a pod thing, where each pod was twenty-five square feet," he explains. "So inside this warehouse, you have all these pods people can rent to cultivate their medicine. We'd screen everybody—doctors, background checks, the works—and fill it to capacity."

El Machino estimates that he and Hoyt would have been able to post $45,000 to $50,000 per month in profit once it was up and running. "That's just renting pods," he says. For a variety of reasons, he and Hoyt opted to create Green Spot instead, and given that just a week earlier, voters rejected Prop. 19, they made the right business decision. But El Machino is quick to add that he's not just in the marijuana business for the money. As the father of two young children, he says, it pains him to see how California's public-sector infrastructure, especially the state's school system, is collapsing under the weight of the implosion of the real-estate market and the ongoing global economic recession. Marijuana can solve all the Golden State's woes if just given a proper chance.

"Legalize it, tax it, and get the schools back open—the student programs, the band, the athletics—get all that back," he says. "I see teachers getting red slips, losing their jobs, getting their hours cut, having to go out on their own to buy pencils and paper. Let's seriously get our priorities straight here."

El Machino lowers his voice. "Then you've got the cartels," he continues. "I am very careful what I say about those guys, but the reality is that 80 percent of their drug business is marijuana, and the majority of their marijuana comes up to the United States." While American taxpayers spend billions trying to destroy America's biggest cash crop, the Mexicans are waiting in the wings, ready to flood the marketplace with their inferior product. "They're smuggling it in and then they've got ninety million acres in Humboldt, and if the sheriff comes in they shoot him on sight—all that crazy stuff."

At the mention of Humboldt, Lucky's ears prick up, and he begins to narrate a story that I will hear several more times in the next few months, what pot smugglers call their "close-call" story. For Lucky, the close-call story involves the time he and a friend are driving down the hill from one of their pot farms in the Emerald Triangle and are pulled over by Mendocino County Sheriff's deputies. In between them, in the front of the car, is a big jar full of weed. The deputies walk up to side of the car and smell the weed.

"You got weed in the car?" the deputy asks Lucky, who says yes and shows the cop the jar of weed.

"You got any in the trunk?" he continues, not even bothering to check out the jar.

"I got nothing," Lucky responds.

"You mind if I look?" says the deputy, and then he gives Lucky a breakdown of what's going to happen next. "You got fifteen pounds in there, you're fine," he explains. "If you got twenty, I have to give you a ticket. Anything over twenty, we've got problems."

Hoyt and El Machino—even Glew—are rolling their eyes in disbelief.

"That's exactly what he said, dude," Lucky insists. "Ninety percent of the staff up in Mendocino are city cops from down here and L.A. At this time of the year, every scandalous cop in the industry goes up to Mendocino because they are the number-one pirates. They take more weed from the growers than anybody and don't report it. They're doing that up there right now."

"So what happened?" El Machino asks.

"Oh, nothing," Lucky answers. "The trunk was empty."

Unlike Mark Moen, for example, Lucky wasn't relying on luck alone to get him out of the Emerald Triangle without getting busted. Instead, he hauled his pot—all two hundred pounds of it—in another vehicle, the driver of which had no idea what was in the trunk, because he happened to be a tow truck operator. "I loaded up my car, they towed it and just followed me," Lucky explains, laughing and slapping his knee.

"Word," he concludes victoriously. "I'm a fucking modern-day moonshiner!"

8 | Lucky

Before he became a weed runner, Lucky had a different nickname: the Jangler.

That's what his skateboarding friends called him, because of the keys that hung from the carabiner clip attached to his belt. He had a funny habit of jangling them with his fingers right before dropping down a near-vertical ramp. "I grew up smoking weed at a pretty young age," Lucky tells me over breakfast back in Southern California, and it's clear that whatever skateboarding memories he has are completely wrapped up in his rise in stock of general coolness and ultimately his current status as top-of-the-line weed dealer turned medical-marijuana capitalist.

Growing up in the affluent East Bay suburb of Walnut Creek, Lucky hung around other incredibly overprivileged, under-supervised, disaffected rich kids, including Christy Turlington, who was already scoring the occasional modeling gig in San Francisco, and was just on the brink of becoming a supermodel. That's when Turlington ran away from home with two of her sisters and moved into his apartment. Lucky liked her parents enough that he felt compelled to tell them she was with him and would be back in a week or so. Together he and the girls would run off to Berkeley to panhandle in the street, just for kicks. "Between the five of us, after two hours, we'd have fifty dollars," Lucky remembers. "It was a joke, just a fun thing to do. I don't know why we enjoyed it."

Turlington soon set off to Europe, appearing in a music video with Duran Duran and dating bassist John Taylor. Lucky, who never finished high school, also left the Bay Area. He and a buddy who shared a shared passion for weightlifting moved to Los Angeles, hoping to win work as *Playgirl* magazine models. "We were basically going to try to become male gigolos and break into this industry," he says. "But we got down there and we were just laughed at."

At eighteen years old, Lucky explains, he looked too young to pose nude. His life ambitions amounted to what would have looked to perverts and prosecutors alike as child pornography. Instead, Lucky and his friend moved in with a model from Northern California who was living in the Los Feliz Towers apartments just downhill from L.A.'s Griffith Park Observatory. As they soon discovered, the woman was working as a call girl and running counterfeit money.

"She'd take us out to dinners and give us a couple of hundreds to buy drinks and would always say to keep the change," Lucky says. "It was so much money." Lucky quickly realized he and his other friend passing the bills were pawns, whose function was basically to spend the fugazi bills in various nightclubs and risk getting arrested. "She was using us to see how good it worked in the clubs. After we discovered that, we decided to take some, and we always had as much money as we could handle."

The call girl had so much cash on hand that while trying to pursue a modeling career, he not only had free rent but could stay at the nicest hotels and, short of a new car, buy just about any toy he wanted. Unfortunately, he bragged about his fortune—and more recklessly, his host's status as a call girl. Word got back to her. "A day later, I get a call," Lucky says. "You're such an asshole," the model told him. "You better get down here and get your shit out of my apartment. I'm pushing your shit out on the street in a shopping cart."

Newport Beach, where Lucky moved a few days later, was overrun with coke parties in the mid-1980s. For weeks one summer, he lived out of his car, sleeping off hangovers in the backseat or on someone's couch, waking up just in time for the next party. About a week into this dead-end existence, he accidentally bumped into an aggressive surfer, causing him to drop his beer. The surfer demanded Lucky go outside to fight, swung the first punch, and missed. Lucky grabbed him by the face and slammed him into a nearby trunk. Watching the whole thing was another reckless young punk like Lucky named Anthony, who happened to know the surfer Lucky had just laid flat.

The teenager roared up on his motorcycle. "Come on. I live right down the street," he shouted. "Where do you live? You're living with me."

Lucky's new roommate turned out to be the son of a man named Robert "Fat Bobby" Paduano, who was reputed to be the head of the Southern California branch of the Chicago Mafia, which had settled in Newport Beach, wreaking havoc there. Police jokingly referred to the outfit as the "Mickey Mouse Mafia," in reference to its Disneyland environs. One of the people who often crashed at the house was one of the mob chief's rumored enforcers, who was typically passed out on the couch with his gun in his belt. "For the three or four months I lived there," Lucky recalls, "they were doing the craziest shit. They were out robbing cocaine dealers and shit."

In fact, Lucky had stumbled right into the middle of one of the most colorful chapters of the history of organized crime in Southern California. Newport Beach in the late 1980s saw a string of assassinations, professional and otherwise, within several months, spotlighting the city's status as a playground (and killing field) for shady businessmen, drug kingpins, and organized-crime figures affiliated with the Mickey Mouse Mafia, who reveled in Newport Beach's glamorous lifestyle and coke-fueled nightlife scene.

On January 1, 1987, forty-eight-year-old Jimmy Lee Casino, the owner of the Mustang Topless Theater, a Santa Ana strip club, returned to his Buena Park home after attending a New Year's Eve party with his twenty-two-year-old girlfriend. As the *Los Angeles Times* later reported, two "masked and armed intruders were waiting. The intruders tied up and raped his girlfriend and dragged Casino downstairs. They ransacked the condo, taking jewelry, furs, credit cards, and two cars." Then they shot Casino three times in the head. (In May 2008, police arrested Richard C. Morris Jr. at his home in Oahu, Hawaii, and charged him in connection with the shooting.)

Casino, whose real name was James Lee Stockwell, was a well-known mobster with a three-decades-long rap sheet, the *Times* wrote. He wasn't the last person connected with the Mustang to find himself on the wrong end of a gun. On May 1, 1987, local mobsters Joseph Angelo Grosso and Michael Anthony Rizzitello forced Bill Carroll, one of the strip club's investors, to a Costa Mesa parking garage. The two men were angry because Carroll had barred them from the club for selling cocaine. They shot him through the face, blinding him, but he survived. Both men were convicted of attempted murder and sent to prison, where Rizzitello later died. (In January 1988, the Mustang, which had survived earlier, unsolved arson attempts, mysteriously burned to the ground.)

Just six days after the attempted hit on Carroll, Joe Avila, a Mexican-American restaurateur whose family still owes the Avila's El Ranchito chain in Southern California, was driving his Porsche in an unincorporated area near Newport Beach when someone blew him away with automatic weapons fire. Police had long suspected Avila of being involved in drug smuggling with certain ex-affiliates of the Brotherhood of Eternal Love, and that either Mafia hit-men or Colombian cartel assassins had murdered him. Aside from the bullets, all they found at the scene was a discarded motorcycle.

Meanwhile, between late 1986 and early 1988, it seemed as though every cocaine dealer in Newport Beach was being ripped off by a trio of Samoan mob enforcers led by Johnny Matua. Between August 1987 and March 1988, Deputy DA Wallace Wade probed the robberies—none of which had been reported to police—and put a string of witnesses on the stand before a grand jury in an attempt to implicate Paduano in the crimes. Each of the robbery victims, all of whom unconvincingly claimed they had nothing to do with the coke business, alleged that Matua had shown up at their front door carrying flowers, only to pull out a gun, steal whatever cash was lying around, and then leave with a demand they either work for Paduano or get out of Newport Beach. One of the last witnesses to take the stand was George Yudzevich, a former Mustang bouncer who had recently turned state's evidence against the Mafia in a federal case in New York. He repeatedly attempted to plead the Fifth, but then reluctantly answered several questions. On March 16, 1988, someone shot Yudzevich to death at a business park in Irvine. Both Paduano and Matua were convicted of the robberies and sent to prison for several years.

"Those were crazy days," recalls Lucky. "Fat Bobby's son Anthony was fucking crazy. After I moved in, he and I were off and running, getting in fights, causing shit everywhere." One morning, about four months into his stay at the house, Lucky was awoken when several Newport Beach police officers came flying through the windows. They searched the entire house with drug-sniffing dogs, and put everyone in separate rooms. "The cops warned me to move out. They straight up told me to get out, that I should not be living there, but I loved those guys, and they loved me, because I was a fighter."

A modeling gig in Europe provided an escape route. He lived in Italy for a year modeling for Emilio Cavallini and other brands before returning to the Bay Area to work as a design consultant for Levi Strauss. "I gave them a whole bunch of insight into their product line," he claims. "One of the ladies in upper management suggested I seek royalties because I was contributing a lot more than I was expected to, and when I did that, I found myself out of a job."

Lucky landed a six-figure Nintendo commercial, which allowed him to start his own fashion line. He founded his own fashion label, which we'll call B. Lucky, in 1990. Before long, the B. Lucky logo was on stiff-brim ball caps and T-shirts worn by skaters throughout California. "I was friends with all the skaters up and down the coast," he said. "It was the raddest vibe. I was skateboarding, and hanging out, getting in a lot of trouble."

During that time, he sponsored a generation of up-and-coming skaters, including Christian Hosoi, who went on to become a world-famous skateboarder before falling into drug abuse and eventually being arrested and sent to federal prison for smuggling. He also promoted up-and-coming Bay Area bands such as Primus, which would often play at his Oakland warehouse. This is when Lucky leveraged his connections with the extreme sports and music world to become a successful weed dealer. His timing and location couldn't have been better. In the early 1990s, Lucky explains, graduate students in botany at the nearby University of California, Berkeley, were engaging in some extracurricular research. They took a sativa plant from an outdoor grower in Humboldt and began experimenting with it. For lack of a better name, they called it the Builder.

"The reason they called it the Builder was the way that it grew was so particular," Lucky tells me. "They would cluster together and build on top of each other almost like building blocks." Very few people were privy to the genetics of the original plant, but its fame quickly spread once a small group of botanists began creating strains from Builder mother plants. "If you give this plant to five different botanists, it will be grown five different ways and you will get five different results," he explains. "Somebody in New York started growing it and changed the name to the Diesel, and then someone else doing the same thing called their strain Chem Dog, but they were really offshoots of the Builder from Berkeley."

One of Lucky's good friends was one of the original marketers of the Builder. "He wasn't the genetics engineer but just a friendly guy who knew dudes in botany class. He was a stoner, and into snowboarding, and knew how to deal weed and how to stack money."

Lucky and his friends benefited not just from their botanical expertise but also from bands such as Primus, who had stoner entourages and who could help popularize and market the Builder strain through time-tested branding strategies. "That's why now, all the Chem Dogs and Sour Diesels have the genetics of this Builder strain," Lucky says.

Lucky's friend did well with his gardens over the years. Most of his money is now invested in other properties: a restaurant in Oakland, a sandwich shop, and a couple of cleaning businesses. "He's got steady income—each of these businesses makes five, ten, fifteen grand a month, and it's all legitimate, and now, all of a sudden, everything makes sense, because we were some of the first guys that were privileged enough to enjoy and experience the Builder before anyone else got in on it."

One afternoon during the Builder era, Lucky was watching television when he saw the famous rapper Ice-T wearing a No Fear hat. He couldn't believe a rapper of such reputation would wear such gear. "This guy is one of the most hardcore guys in the world and he's wearing the gayest clothing," he told himself. "I have to find him now."

Ice-T was playing at the Lollapalooza show in a few weeks, so Lucky bought a dozen tickets and showed up at the concert, along with his entire company team, in full B. Lucky gear. After talking himself backstage, Lucky ran up to the rapper and introduced himself. "You can't wear that," he said. "Take that shit off."

Instead of kicking his ass, Ice-T turned to one of his assistants and ordered him to get Lucky's contact information. Lucky then bullshitted his way into a radio station in Colorado that was promoting a local Lollapalooza skate jam, and used the airplay to falsely claim that he was now handling Ice-T's official wardrobe. As soon as the segment ended, he and his entourage appeared at the event gate with several large duffel bags full of B. Lucky gear. But lacking passes, security refused them admission. After a few minutes, a bus pulled up and began emptying members of Ice-T's hip-hop crew, the Rhyme Syndicate. Lucky began running alongside them as they walked into the show.

"Hey, bro," Lucky said to the biggest of the bunch, a six-foot-eight-inch-tall heavyweight. "This is Ice-T's personal gear." Just then, one of the security guards caught up with Lucky and tried to pull him back outside. Lucky threatened to drop all of the clothing on the ground if he wasn't allowed in, adding that whoever stopped him from entering would have to explain everything to Ice-T. "Hold up a minute," said the biggest guy in the rapper's entourage. "Y'all wait here. Let me go get Ice."

Five minutes later, the star walked up to Lucky, dripping with sweat from his interrupted workout session. Lucky began talking before Ice-T could say a word, reminding the rapper that they'd met in California. "Hold up," Ice said to the security guards. "These guys are with me. Take all this shit into my dressing room." Inside, members of the Rhyme Syndicate started pulling open the bags, and Ice-T picked out several hats and shirts for himself. "This shit is OG," Ice declared. "This is badass."

About a month after the show, Ice-T called up Lucky and invited him to run his new clothing line. For the next decade, Lucky worked for a series of companies and startup enterprises in the extreme-sports world, typically coming up with promotional concepts and then selling the ideas to investors, using the cash to seed his next endeavor. "But all along, ever since back in the day, I was still selling weed," he admits. "That's how I had so many friends. We'd smoke, I'd sell a little weed, and then all of a sudden, I'd have another business venture. I'd sell a little more weed and then all of a sudden I had more investors and partners and a new idea to launch."

In the mid-2000s, after twenty years of developing his nationwide network of business contacts and high-end pot customers, Lucky was ready to get into the marijuana industry full time. He'd kept in touch with his friends from the Builder days. "These guys had grown so much in the pot world," he says. "They went from selling pounds to tens of pounds, to hundreds of pounds to thousands of pounds, from citywide to statewide to nationwide and international." Like Lucky, many of his friends had used their weed money to fund legitimate businesses. "That's how the entire rap industry was built," Lucky observes. "It all came from the streets."

A major factor in Lucky's decision to go into the legitimate marijuana industry was the presidential candidacy of Barack Obama, a known stoner in high school and college who signaled during the campaign that he had no intention of standing in the way of states such as California that had legalized pot for medicinal use. Lucky opened his collective, as well as an online marijuana cultivation school by the same name, and even a weed-centric magazine, within months of Obama's election.

But arguably the biggest reason behind his move to open a dispensary, Lucky claims, was witnessing his mother fall ill with breast cancer and endure a double masectomy. Having survived the ordeal, she credited her mental stability to smoking marijuana.

Lucky recalls going to a 2009 city council meeting where Lake Forest officials were debating how to handle the proliferation of cannabis clubs. He felt a mixture of pride and relief to take a public stand on something that he'd been involved in for so long in the underground economy. "God forbid any of you wind up with cancer, or your wives or children," he said. "That, I guarantee you, will change your attitude, without question."

But even as Lucky entered the quasi-legitimate world of the medical-marijuana industry, he continued making money the old-fashioned, and much-more-profitable way: pot smuggling. Along the way, he built alliances with a broad array of associates in organized crime, players that continue to play a hidden role in the underground economy of marijuana cultivation and transportation, players with names like the Hells Angels and the Irish Mafia. Perhaps the most unusual—and ultimately tragic—operation he pulled off involved both those groups and also smugglers from the Mohawk Nation whose reservation straddled the US-Canada border, as well as a hip-hop artist from Montreal nicknamed Bad News Brown.

— — — — —

Bad News Brown, who was born Paul Frappier in Haiti in 1977, is most widely known as a harmonica-playing MC. But when he wasn't opening concerts for Snoop Dogg, Kanye West, or 50 Cent, Frappier was dealing marijuana in Montreal, where the Hells Angels controlled the marijuana market.

"The Hells Angels own Montreal," says Lucky, comparing the club's presence there to what he witnessed in Oakland as a kid growing up in the 1960s. "Eighty percent of the club's entire membership is in Montreal. I've watched these guys take over streets in Montreal—whole streets, no questions asked." While there was plenty of opportunity to make cash selling weed in Montreal, the challenge for Frappier and his Hells Angels cohorts was finding enough high-quality product to meet the demand. That's where Lucky came in.

Someone with the biker club in Montreal talked to a comrade in Southern California, who in turn talked to a mutual friend of Lucky, an Irishman, who set up a meeting at a pub in Huntington Beach on St. Patrick's Day. Without mentioning Frappier by name, the Irishman explained—over a round of Harp Lagers, their conversation muted by a Pogues album blasting from the jukebox—that he had a Canadian contact capable of unloading multi-hundred-pound quantities of marijuana. All Lucky needed to do was get himself to Montreal for a tête-à-tête. Accompanied by a friend who rode along for protection, he boarded a flight from Los Angeles International Airport to Montreal, but upon landing in Canada, immigration authorities refused to allow him entry in to the country because he had been arrested there several years earlier—unfortunate baggage from his days as a barroom brawler.

Lucky and his friend quickly found themselves on a one-way flight to Atlanta, Georgia, on which they got insanely drunk while awaiting instructions from their Irish friend, who would put them in touch with the Mohawk smugglers. "The Indians on this reservation, they smuggle eighty thousand cigarettes an hour into the United States, and all over the place," Lucky explains. "My Irish friend told us to get the fuck up there and don't worry about it, these guys are doing to do whatever needs to be done to get us there."

So that afternoon, Lucky and his friend boarded a flight to New York City and drove to Vermont, then boarded a ferry across Lake Champlain to upstate New York, where, well after dark, they arrived at their rendezvous point, a gas station on the Akwesasne Mohawk reservation, which straddles the US-Canada border along the St. Lawrence River, an area known as "Smugglers Alley." There, fast boats and Jet Skis bearing loads of contraband—untaxed alcohol and cigarettes, drugs, firearms, and cash—dodge Coast Guard and border patrol vessels all year until the water freezes over, at which point snowmobiles take to the ice.

Lucky and his friend had been warned not to drive onto the reservation, but to take an Indian taxi instead. As they rode in, they passed road signs that had been spray-painted with various threats and epithets directed at the US government, the most popular being Fuck FBI. The cabdriver explained that the roads were the site of countless car chases between state troopers and Mohawks fleeing for sovereign land in their Land Rovers and Lamborghinis. The tit-for-tat game had recently escalated, the cabbie added, when a female trooper had been kidnapped and left hanging naked but otherwise unharmed thirty feet high up a telephone pole.

The taxi left Lucky and his friend at the gas station and disappeared. Fifteen minutes later, several Mohawks pulled up in a separate car and brought the pair down to the water. Waiting for them on the shore was a cigarette boat that had been spray-painted black, with twin 500 Mercury engines. The driver wore a motorcycle helmet, night-vision goggles, and a bulletproof vest. He told Lucky and his friend to hold tight, and raced across the water in pitch dark, running the vessel aground on the gentle slope of a lawn in someone's backyard. After paying the driver, Lucky and his friend jumped into the backseat of a black Ford Expedition driven by a middle-aged Indian man whose wife sat in the passenger seat. They reached Montreal by sunrise.

That evening, Lucky met with several Irish mob and Hells Angels representatives as well as Frappier, who had access to what he described as high-grade hydroponic marijuana. "He was a super cool guy, a badass harmonica player," Lucky recalls. "He thought he could hook us up with all this weed." Lucky's role was to use his connections with dispensaries and other parties to broker the best deal he could for the pot. But when the product arrived in the US, following the same smuggling route that Lucky used to get himself to Montreal, it turned out to be inferior, and Lucky couldn't sell half of the agreed-upon amount. He never talked to Frappier again, but knew that the misbegotten venture had engendered some very bad blood between him and the bikers. "I don't know what they wound up doing," Lucky says. "But four months later, Bad News Brown wound up dead. It's so sad; he had a two-and-a-half-year-old baby."

Lucky said he has no knowledge of those responsible for the murder, but speculates that Frappier's fate could have been set in motion by the failed marijuana scheme, and perhaps sealed by something Frappier did or said when confronted about it. "He might have said the wrong thing to the wrong guy," he adds. "Usually the nicest, calmest little dudes have really gnarly friends. Ninety percent of the time, in my experience, you really have no idea who you're dealing with."

According to the *Toronto Sun*, a passerby discovered Frappier's body on the street, near some abandoned buildings adjacent to the Lachine Canal in southwestern Montreal early in the morning on February 11, 2011. He'd been severely beaten and shot in the back of the head; the police had no motive or suspects.

– – – – –

Lucky's closest call as a smuggler happened shortly after Frappier's murder. A friend who was working with an Emerald Triangle marijuana grower fronted him one hundred pounds, which Lucky planned to sell in Chicago for a tidy profit of $130,000. He and a friend posed as a pair of roadies who were caravanning in a car and truck full of sound equipment that was needed for a gig in the Windy City. "We made a crate that we could seal up with all the weed in it and loaded it into the car," Lucky explains. "We had walkie-talkies so we could talk to each other on the road." Despite such preparation, the pair made a series of entirely preventable errors. First, they were driving west along Interstate 80, the biggest smuggling route in the United States, with California plates. "We should have switched plates in Utah or Colorado," Lucky explains. "Also, our orders were to drive straight through, never stop in the same place together, and never talk to anybody, and we ended up picking up this girl on the side of the freeway who [was] doing speed."

After driving all night, the pair pulled off to get gas in rural Nebraska, and ate breakfast at the café next to the truck stop. It was only after they sat down, bleary-eyed, and began eating their omelets that they realized they'd stopped in a one-horse town where most of the men sitting at the tables were either cops or city workers whose brothers or fathers were cops or judges, or for that matter, the mayor. All eyes watched as they ate their eggs. "It was getting weirder and weirder," Lucky says. "We get up to pay and walk to our cars, and my friend opens the door to the truck and you can smell the weed." Instead of driving away, Lucky's friend went back into the restaurant and, in front of everyone, purchased a pine-tree-shaped air freshener to mask the scent.

Not more than ten miles down the road, with the two vehicles driving about a mile apart, Lucky passed a state trooper coming from the other direction. The patrol car made a quick U-turn, hit the siren, and pulled behind him. The cop appeared to know that Lucky was caravanning with another vehicle; Lucky told him their cover story, that they were carrying concert equipment to Chicago. The cop put Lucky and the girl in the back of his car, and while the officer fruitlessly searched Lucky's car for drugs, Lucky heard over the cop's radio that the police had found the stash in his friend's truck.

Immediately, the speed-freak girl began sobbing. "She's crying and screaming, having the whole tweaker meltdown," Lucky recalls. The cop takes them all to the station. "My friend comes from a wealthy family in Irvine and has never been arrested, and now we're looking at doing fifteen to twenty years in Nebraska." Both he and his friend stuck to their story, refusing to acknowledge under relentless questioning that they knew anything about the marijuana sealed inside the equipment. The girl, meanwhile, turned out to be the daughter of a high-ranking US military officer who was serving in Iraq. "She's yelling at the cops to get on the red phone and call her dad," Lucky says. "Get the fucking red phone! I figured this bitch was going to get us all put in the loony bin, but sure enough they call the dad and the next thing you know, it's 'yes sir, we have your daughter here, sir, yes sir, no sir.'"

After the cops cut their passenger loose, Lucky and his friend made bail. The charges were eventually dropped when the cops failed to provide any justifiable cause for the stop. He still marvels at the fact that the police apparently never tested the stash area for his fingerprints. "It would have been all over for me if they'd just said they had my fingerprints on the pot," he insists. "I'm sure I'd have confessed. But they never did."

Meanwhile, Lucky had just lost $130,000 or more worth of confiscated marijuana, and even though the charges didn't stick, his troubles were far from over. What Lucky didn't know until after he lost the load was that the pot had belonged to the Hells Angels, who weren't going to wait long to collect their cash.

Lucky talked to an intermediary and offered to set up another deal to repay the money. He was told to wait for an answer, and be open-minded about how he might have to atone for the bust. A few weeks went by, during which time Lucky procured a stolen handgun. "I'm getting sick every day, convinced somebody is going to show up and tell me that I have to kill somebody, take a name and address, and not ask a fucking question. I didn't eat for two weeks without throwing up, trying to convince myself that whoever I'd be told to kill would be some piece-of-shit rapist or fucking child abuser, so I wouldn't feel any remorse, like a normal person."

The knock on the front door of his suburban Orange County house came late one weekday morning. Lucky was taking a shower upstairs. He looked down from the top of the staircase though a moon-shaped window at someone's rather large chest, which was decorated with a prominent Orange County motorcycle club logo. "This is a nice little neighborhood with kids, and these guys are both decked out with their patches in full effect, so I opened the door and told them to come inside right away," Lucky says. Before the two men could say a word, Lucky explained that he'd procured a gun and was ready to kill whomever they asked. The bikers looked at each other, eyebrows raised. "No, no, no," one of them protested. "Back up. Stop. We don't want any of that."

Meanwhile, Lucky's cell phone is ringing nonstop. "I probably took two out of ten calls," he says. "One from Ice-T and one from a business partner of mine who owns a big toy company." When Lucky finished his calls, the bikers told him that all they wanted from him was help promoting their rallies, getting bands to play, and finding legitimate ways they could raise money for the club. "Are you fucking kidding me?" Lucky asked. "That's all you want me to do? Make a few flyers and promote some fucking events?"

Since the visit, he's occasionally had to field favors from the club, such as getting them backstage for an Ice-T concert. But the club has also come in handy, like when Lucky's ex-wife started going downhill, living with a drug dealer in Los Angeles and getting strung out. The bikers rode up north, scared her friends away, and told her that she wasn't allowed to hang out with them anymore.

"They've been very helpful," Lucky says. "They don't want to see me stressed out. Now, I'm their golden goose."

9 | Cameras

The California Highway Patrol car heading south sees us about five minutes after the rain stops, just as the sun pokes through the mist.

The patrol car pulls a U-turn and hits the siren. Lucky starts laughing uncontrollably, slapping his thigh and shaking his head, completely unconcerned about the pound or so of marijuana in the carry-on bag that's laying on the backseat.

"Welcome to the Emerald Triangle, dude," he says, shaking his head. "Highest concentration of speed traps in the world."

This is certainly going to be the end of my wonderful road trip to Lucky's pot farm in the heart of America's underground marijuana economy. At least the rain, which has followed us all the way from the airport at Oakland, has finally stopped.

"License and registration," the cop demands.

I hand the cop my driver's license and rental paperwork. My voice is shaking slightly as I realize that our car reeks with the scent of weed. This fact hasn't gone unnoticed by Lucky, who is smiling and nodding his head in a ridiculous way.

"You're from Southern California," the cop observes. "What brings you gentlemen up here this morning?"

"Ah," I say, "just visiting some friends for the weekend?"

That was not supposed to sound like a question.

The cop takes a deep breath, dramatically inhaling the aroma. Seconds, each one a lifetime, pass in silence. Without so much as a wink, he walks back to his patrol car. A few minutes later, he returns, hands me my speeding ticket, and says nothing about the obvious stench of weed. Nor does he demand to search the car.

The cop's eyes dart to the rear of the car. He looks at Lucky.

"Yep, just visiting friends," Lucky repeats, smiling broadly.

I'm not sure what I've just witnessed, but nothing about what just happened makes sense to me. Why hasn't the cop already said something about the pot stench in our car? Why aren't we being led out of the vehicle in handcuffs? I look over at Lucky and it's obvious he's cracking up. Later, he will tell me that it took all his willpower not to tell the cop that I was a reporter writing about the Emerald Triangle and we are on our way to visit an illegal pot farm.

"Have fun," the cop says. "And watch your speed."

– – – – –

Lucky isn't nervous driving with pot in his car inside the Triangle. He's gotten over that fear a long time ago, and if anything, he enjoys the risk.

Between October 15 and December 15, Lucky explains, roughly four out of every ten cars on the road is loaded down with marijuana, and both the freeway and the small towns it crosses are crawling with narcs. They're watching the hotels, where East Coast buyers stay for a week before blowing through half a million bucks, arranging pot deals, as well as the gas stations and car washes. "You never want to drive into town with mud all over your truck," he says. "That's a sign right there that you've just driven off the mountain, and that's probable cause. That's the first lesson of coming off the mountain: Clean your car. And never fucking stay at one of the shitty motels in town; they're crawling with undercover cops. It's so stupid that people think it's cool to do that."

Having made the trip south to Orange County more times than he can remember, Lucky has learned all the secrets to successfully smuggling weed, which is why he hasn't been caught. "You get your truck loaded down—I would never go over 150 or 200 pounds—and you get the fuck off the mountain at 4:30 in the morning on a Monday, and you're in the rush-hour traffic headed to work," he says. "There are so many thousands of cars on the roads that their odds of being able to pick somebody are just shattered, and your odds of getting through are that much more increased. Drive the speed limit and try to stay close to cars that are shady-looking—teenagers, kids, anyone who looks more suspicious than you."

By now, I've grown accustomed to Lucky's strange, playful way with people, his incredible ease in handling stressful situations and making everyone feel relaxed. He carries himself with the confidence of a man who just knows he will never get caught, no matter how high the risk. While seemingly everyone I've met while covering the medical-marijuana movement has had nothing but grief from the law, perhaps by being too naïve about the consequences, Lucky effortlessly rose to the top of the medical-marijuana industry with his own rather huge collective, and then, at just the right time, he bailed out of the business and made a killing by selling his operation off to a rich Republican who subsequently lost his entire investment.

This was a guy so sure of himself that he'd managed to convince a web of legal corporations—manufacturers and distributors of everything from soil nutrients to greenhouse hardware, lights, and other growing equipment—to provide him with free supplies for his and his friends' various pot farms in Mendocino and Humboldt counties. In return for the goods, Lucky agreed to document his harvests by taking photographs and even digital movies of the growing operations he helped manage for various marijuana-focused magazines and websites—call it free product placement, Emerald Triangle style.

Which is why when Lucky asked his ex-girlfriend, a sales and marketing rep for one such magazine, to bring a duffel bag full of video cameras from Southern California, she didn't immediately think he was crazy for saying he planned to spend the weekend documenting life at one of his farms. Lucky asked her to do this because she was already driving up north with a couple of her girlfriends. They planned to spend the weekend in the mountains of Northern California trimming weed at Lucky's farm in exchange for several hundred dollars in salary and all the pot they could smoke, plus a nice gift bag of weed when they left.

The trip took place two years ago, at the beginning of harvest season in early October. The girl—we'll call her Amber—picked up her passenger, a blonde beauty from Newport Beach who almost sparked a statewide manhunt because she went on the trip without telling her family or any of her other friends. The pair's next stop was picking up Lucky at his home in south Orange County. Suddenly, Lucky called Amber on her cell phone.

"Before we leave," he asked, "can you pick up some video cameras?"

"No problem," answered Amber.

Lucky then instructed Amber to drive to Temecula and meet a friend of his named Nate in a parking lot of a strip mall with a Target and an Applebee's restaurant. On her way to Temecula, Amber received a text message from Nate saying that he would meet her at the strip mall and she would then follow him to a house where the cameras were located. Twenty-five minutes after Amber arrived at the lot, Nate pulled up in his car.

"He's got blond hair, blue eyes, diamond earrings, [is] covered in tattoos, and is driving a brand-new white Cadillac," Amber recalls. "I followed him out of town, and went down this long dirt road with a locked gate at the end of it. The Mexican guy that comes down to the gate has a gun, and on the other side is a huge rooster farm. It was like the Southern California cockfighting headquarters of the Mexican cartels. They have one small cage full of hens; the rest are cocks."

Each rooster had its own one-hundred-gallon blue water reservoir for an enclosure, with a small door cut out at the base and a post inside, to which each rooster was attached by string so it could only walk a foot or two outside the container to see the hens and the other roosters and get mad. "There are four or five mobile homes on stilts, and tons of Hispanic people who didn't speak English," Amber says. Nate, the only white guy present, went inside one of the trailers and returned with three large duffel bags. Ordering Amber to open her trunk, he threw the bags in her car and asked her if she wanted to smoke a joint.

"He throws me this bag of weed and papers," Amber continues. "And I'm shaking. How did I get myself in this situation? And my friend was so ignorant. She was like, 'Why do they have so many roosters?' She had no idea what was going on." After lighting the joint, Amber asked Nate if he wanted to smoke. "Oh no," he answered. "I'm on parole. I just got out of prison three weeks ago."

As she drove away from the rooster farm to pick up Lucky, Amber knew there was no chance that the duffel bags actually contained video cameras as Lucky had said. "I was scared and didn't want to ask what it was," she says. "I was thinking of pulling over and looking but how scary would that be, to find out? I hauled ass and then realized I can't be speeding, because who knows what I have in my car." After sticking to the speed limit back to Orange County, Amber picked up Lucky, who immediately asked to see the bags in the trunk. "What's in there?" Amber asked. "Does it matter?" Lucky asked. "It's easier if you don't know, right?"

After picking up another cute friend of Amber's who also wanted to make some quick cash trimming weed over the weekend, Lucky volunteered to drive north, but when they stopped to get gas in L.A., he asked Amber to drive, knowing full well that since it was her car, and she was driving it, she'd be held responsible if the cops found anything illegal inside. Amber drove all the way to San Francisco without incident; Lucky then instructed her to drive to a friend's house. He grabbed the bags out of the trunk and left Amber and her friends to wait for him in the car.

"What was in the bags?" she asked when Lucky returned.

"Dirt weed from Mexico," said Lucky.

"We just drove weed to Northern California?" Amber marveled aloud. "That doesn't make any sense."

"Yes, it does," Lucky insisted. "They don't have that crap up here. There's a market for it."

In fact, Amber had just helped Lucky transport twenty-five pounds of Mexican brick weed that had been smuggled from Mexico to Temecula by the cartels. Lucky saw an easy way to make $15,000—that's $600 per pound—by unloading it to friends in Frisco who, in turn, would sell it to the local street gangs. For her troubles, Amber earned an extra $500.

Later that night, they finally reached Lucky's friend's pot farm in Mendocino County. Already staying at the house was the core growing crew: a horticulturist and three workers who, especially during the outdoor growing season, rarely left the farm and got maybe one or two days off per month. They hadn't seen any girls in weeks, and Lucky quickly became a celebrity for having brought a trio of such attractive trimmers with him.

There were several guest tents set up in the grass next to the greenhouses, but Lucky, ever the gentleman, invited Amber's two friends to sleep in the master bedroom since the owner was away that night. After everyone settled down to sleep, the two girls got in their pajamas and were about to doze off when a stark naked Lucky jumped in between them. "Hi, girls," he said, winking. "It's time to cuddle!"

Amber could hear their screams from her tent. She ran into the house, and they were already downstairs, shaking with anger. Amber confronted Lucky, who was still in bed upstairs, not visibly upset that his attempt at a threesome had been rebuffed.

"What the fuck?" she asked.

Lucky shrugged his shoulders.

"There's no free lunch," he explained.

— — — — —

I got my first taste of Lucky's ability to work the angles on the day I met him, as the sun set on my afternoon with Chris Glew, Hoyt, and El Machino of the Green Spot delivery service. An hour after we left Glew and the Green Spot boys behind so the trio could test drive El Machino's fleet of Harleys in the nearby hills, I'd driven Lucky to the Marriott Hotel in downtown Oakland. Unbeknownst to Glew or me, Lucky hadn't simply flown north to hang out with me and Glew, but rather to arrange a deal at the Marriott with his friend, a graduate student at UCLA who was waiting for Lucky at the hotel bar, hoping to score $50,000 worth of weed.

The friend had driven up to the Bay Area with the cash in his trunk, enough to buy twenty pounds of medical-grade marijuana. For a fee, Lucky planned to drive up to the Emerald Triangle with his friend and broker the deal. "He's been shipping weed all across the US and is up here purchasing," Lucky told me as we drove through downtown Oakland, explaining that the pot in question can be purchased for $3,000 a pound in the Triangle and then sold for $4,000 to $4,500 on the East Coast. "He's just getting into this and is a little nervous though, a little paranoid," Lucky continued. One could easily imagine being nervous carrying twenty pounds of pot, but to Lucky that's nothing to worry about. "He's a legal patient, so legally, in California, he can have twenty or thirty pounds, justifiably," he said. "It's legally defensible."

Lucky's cell phone rang; he hit the speaker button.

"Hello, sir," Lucky said. "I'm going to head up tonight. We'll get things handled tonight."

"How many?" the caller asked.

"Probably twenty or thirty."

"I have to make a phone call and call you back."

"Okay, call me at the office," Lucky said, the joke being that he doesn't have one.

A few minutes later, we pulled into the Marriott. A Filipino valet approached my rental. Turns out if we want to visit the bar, we'll have to pay twenty-five dollars to park the car. Lucky had another plan. Tapping his cap with a nod, he introduced himself, and began to spin a likely story: his grandmother is at the hotel bar, drunk off her ass, in danger of falling off a stool or some such disaster. We've come to rescue her before she causes any problems. We just need to park for a few minutes so we can get her out of the hotel, and it'd be better for everyone if she left sooner rather than later.

The story is as absurd as it sounds, and Lucky, who was still stoned from our afternoon smoke-out with the Green Spot guys, was having a hard time containing his laughter as he elaborated about the glorious state of grandma's inebriation. For a few moments, it seemed as if Lucky's mind trick is working and he might be able to hypnotize the confused-looking valet into letting us park for free. But no such luck.

"You smoke weed?" Lucky suddenly asked.

"Sometimes."

"That's a political answer," Lucky pointed out.

"Yeah, man, I smoke," the valet admitted sheepishly, at which point Lucky reached into his knapsack and pulled out about an eighth of an ounce of high-grade weed, handing it to our new friend, who quickly agreed to watch the car while we went up to the bar. Lucky's friend turned out to be a Russian who, stereotypically, wore a tracksuit, a close shave, and a gold chain around his neck. Just as Lucky had warned me, the guy looked nervous. Over drinks, we learned that the friend had made a rookie error. He'd actually driven north in his own car, and worse, it was a Mercedes. Because the plan had been to drive north to the Triangle tonight, Lucky wanted to ditch the Benz and use my rental car for the trip. "You can't be driving around the Triangle in the middle of the night in a Mercedes full of weed," he told me.

Earlier, I'd asked Glew, hypothetically of course, what risks were involved with tagging along with Lucky for a run into the Triangle. "Well, it's Northern California, so the worst thing that can happen is you get maybe six months in jail," he'd responded. "That's not my deal. Seriously, good luck with that one. You're in God's hands."

My plan had been to follow behind Lucky and his friend in my rental, so that if anything happened on the trip in and out of the Triangle, I could make a quick getaway—or at least have some kind of plausible deniability. Now, I was facing the prospect of being an accessory to Lucky's twenty-pound drug deal. I'd already been worried enough about tagging along for this escapade, but there's no chance I would let Lucky use my car—rental or otherwise—to stash that kind of weight, much less with me in the vehicle.

I said good-bye to Lucky, and, superfluously, wished him luck.

10 | Let There Be Light

It has been raining steadily for days, but the evening sun now pierces the haze like a pink, flaming orb, its broken rays angling downward through a gallery of thirty-foot-high windows recently carved into a towering wall of redwoods along the riverbank.

The trees are maybe thirty years old, new-growth trees just a few feet wide at the base but already sixty feet tall. A century ago, the entire valley had been clear-cut by loggers, the lumber stacked like wet cordwood on the flat cars of a southbound train whose long-abandoned tracks now lay below the ridge, rusting and overgrown with weeds. All that remains of the lumber-extraction operation besides the tracks is a railroad bridge that crosses high above the creek. Although the trestles are still sturdy enough to support the weight of a car, there's no road leading to the abandoned structure, and in any case, the ties are rotting in the perpetual dampness.

Like dragon's breath in an illustrated children's book, smoky tendrils of after-rain mist swirl up the steep hillside on the opposite bank of a gully whose ancient creek drains into the main river below. Atop a wide swath of grassy slope stands a house with a wraparound deck. Everywhere in the sky are fine sawdust particles wafting down from the treetops, refracting the dazzling sunlight as they descend. The chain saws and wood chipper are silent now; the staccato slap of water against shoal echoes from the fast-running river, swollen from a month-long inundation. Even though its foundation lies one hundred yards or so uphill from the river, the house has a flood-compliant basement for a first floor. Twice, in the 1950s and 1960s, the river flooded out entire towns in this valley; today, few houses or cabins still stand.

Below the house is a trailer, where a tree-trimming crew from Santa Cruz bunked last night, and a wooden shack near the river that has a stone fireplace on its front porch bisected by the trunk of a sturdy redwood. In the middle of the clearing, between the cabin and the main house, is a trio of sixty-foot-by-thirty-foot greenhouses rigged with a pulley system so that the roof or walls can be rolled up or down at a moment's notice. Inside each structure, row upon row of five-foot-high marijuana plants—four-month-old clones of a high-end Sour Diesel strain created by graduates of UC Berkeley's botany department—sway in the breeze.

The farm is one of at least a dozen outdoor growing operations in Humboldt and Mendocino counties that are either owned by Lucky or by one of his associates, in which case Lucky gets a share of the profits in return for helping distribute the harvest. In addition to the regular outdoor growing season each summer, this farm typically produces three separate indoor crops per year by using powerful grow lights inside the greenhouses.

My journey here with Lucky had started a day earlier, and had nearly been derailed thanks to that speeding ticket in Ukiah. About an hour after our run-in with the cop, we hit Willits, California, the hometown of the world-famous Skunk Train and the birthplace of the Protopipe, a small, metal contraption that allows you to store a gram of pot in a chamber that screws into the pipe and is held in place by a small poker that you can pull out and push into the holes in the bottom of the bowl in order to clean it. After dining on pizza at a restaurant there, we stop by a head shop north of town. The shop reeks of weed, and when we walk in, the red-eyed fellow working the cash register hastily puts out his joint in an ashtray.

Now that we've made it through most of the Triangle, Lucky is eager to purchase a smoking device so he can start puffing once we're back on the road. As he peruses the hundreds of glass pipes on display, he tells the cashier about the cop who was prepared to let him off for carrying anything less than twenty pounds of weed.

The cashier's Latino friend, who is rolling joints on the countertop, curses in disgust. "You have to be fucking white for that to happen," he fumes. "Because that shit does not happen to me. The cops up here will fuck with a local any time of day. The only people he won't pull over are a bunch of dread-headed niggas because he'll know he'll get shot."

The pissed-off joint roller glances over at the cashier. "That shit ever happen to you?" he asks. "Get let go with ten pounds?"

"Fuck no. Never," the cashier responds. "You're lucky you're not from here," he continues. "You're from here and get pulled over with fifteen ounces, and you're going straight to Lodi. You ever spend three nights in a holding cell with no shirt on, dog? Sleeping on concrete? Now, we've got all these fucking people coming here who are filling up the county—all these fools who think marijuana is legal. It may be legal everywhere else, but the reality up here is much more brutal."

Nobody disagrees but the cashier continues anyway. "Listen," he says. "In '09, they came down on my property for fifty-six plants. I have cancer on my neck and gout for life. Me and my partners had three medicals, so it was a legal grow under state law. But they look at me because I'm already fighting a case and they said I shouldn't have more than twenty-five plants. So now I'm only allowed to smoke and take care of myself and sell pipes. That's all I do. They'll take a local boy and roast him over the fire to make an example of him just so all the other locals take a shit. And they rob you, dude. It's not just the cops. I'm sure we got some CIA working out here."

Lucky selects a hookah-shaped pipe with a large glass bowl that can be filled with water and is designed to fit inside a car's beverage holder. As he pays, the cashier offers us some parting words of advice. "My family goes back four generations up here," he begins. "They lived here, they never left, and they're not going away, no matter what comes here or goes from here. There are a lot of people buried in these hills, bro. It's a lot deeper than just fucking scratching the surface, as far as the cops and the robbery and the fucking Mexican cartels go. I wouldn't scratch too deep."

As we get back in the car, Lucky chuckles to himself. "That guy was an idiot," he tells me. "If we were undercover cops, that shop would have been a shut-down shop. We walked in. They have big joints, they were smoking in there, a guy in the back says, 'Do you want to get high?' You cannot refer to the pipes at all for marijuana—period. Then he says, 'Fuck it, you can use it for cocaine, you can stick whatever else you want in it.' And this is all medical, right? Dude, are you fucking kidding me?"

Then again, Lucky is the first one to admit that medical marijuana is more or less a marketing term. Although the farm where we're headed has legal paperwork stating that the marijuana it produces will go to a particular cannabis collective in San Francisco, that's just a ruse to justify transporting the weed to the Bay Area, where much of it will then be shipped further south, to L.A., or to the East Coast.

"I mean the truth is, we say it's for a collective, but we're really selling that shit all around the nation," he says. "I help the harvest by getting free nutrients and stuff like that. I create value that I can bring to the table. In return, I get distribution rights and the right to have some plants in the garden. At this particular place where we're going, I'll probably have ten or twenty plants. At my other spot, I'll have fifty to seventy plants, and in Oroville, I've got a couple hundred more plants."

According to Lucky, Southern California is so inundated with high-quality marijuana that there's not much market for the good stuff there. "We end up selling the weed in New York and make $4,000 or $5,000 a pound," he says. "There are guys that move hundreds of thousands of pounds, in one hundred-pound packs. Selling to a collective, it's just a little deal. You might sell five or ten pounds, and you only make maybe $1,500 a pound, which is why I would say probably only 5 percent of it will actually make it to a medical-marijuana collective."

– – – – –

In the midst of a vast forest twenty miles farther north, Lucky steers around a steep curve, the river two hundred feet below a cliff to our right. He's blowing pot smoke out the driver's-side window as we careen around the bend, pushing 70 mph. A police cruiser is parked on the opposite side of the freeway. Lucky lifts his foot off the accelerator slightly, puts the bong back in the holder, and keeps driving. Thirty seconds later, he screeches to a halt in the gravel on the side of the road.

This time, we're fucked.

Or not.

"Man, I have to wake up," Lucky says, yawning, and suddenly, it's apparent we're not being pulled over. He just figured that this gravelly pitch, where motorists can pull over to check out the view of the river, would make as good a pit stop as any. Lucky sprints back and forth on the roadside until he feels alert, and we continue north.

We pass a hardware store that has a dozen or so trailer-mounted generators parked out front, all of which are going to power greenhouses. The rain, which had cleared up a few hours earlier, begins to fall again. In a forlorn parking lot on the other side of the freeway, a drenched hippie sits on a stool, hawking large Bob Marley and Hello Kitty blankets.

Soon, redwoods with trunks large enough to drive through are towering on either side of the road, blocking out the sun. Farther along, dingy trailers overgrown with weeds stand guard over small, tent-covered marijuana plots just yards from the freeway. As we climb uphill into the mountains, the trees become thinner, replaced with typically golden California grassland. A large red barn crowns one of the hilltops. There's a late-model Ferrari parked next to a satellite dish and an array of radio antennas. "Did you see all that radar shit next to that barn?" Lucky asks me. "That's crazy. They're listening to everybody, keeping an eye on everything."

After zigzagging up and down the backside of a steep mountain, we reach a fern-covered ravine that narrows at a wooden bridge crossing a shallow creek. Waiting for us at the gate is Dave, a recently divorced horticulturalist from New Jersey who jumped at the opportunity to earn a handsome salary living on a pot farm. As is his ritual, Dave, a tall and quiet middle-aged man with long, curly hair, is ending the day the same way he started it: taking his two powerfully built Dobermans on a walk around the property.

Lucky introduces us. "You're going to like him," he says to Dave. "He's a writer. He's going to want to pick your brain."

"Wow," Dave says, raising an eyebrow. "Actual talking."

Dave shuts the gate behind us and follows us up to the main house, which, along with the property and the greenhouses, is owned by one of Lucky's best friends, a pot smuggler from San Francisco named Anton. Like Lucky, he has spent most of the past two decades moving untold tons of weed to the East Coast. Besides smoking pot all day in massive joints rolled from the excess trim from last year's harvest, Anton's job is to cook meals and make sure the fridge is packed and the house is running tight.

At dawn every morning, Dave walks his two dogs and waters the plants. He spends most of the rest of his day tending to individual plants, ensuring each one is healthy. By the time they're ready for trimming, the number of workers on this farm more than quadruples with hourly workers, and the population of the Emerald Triangle itself explodes with an army of trimmers that spend weeks manicuring marijuana branches into ounce after ounce of shelf-ready buds. Until then, it's just Anton, Dave, and Anton's brother Zach, who's permitted to leave the house only once a week—to play golf. He practices his swing each evening by smashing balls into a large tree at the edge of the clearing.

"I've been here since March," Zach says, taking a swing. The ball bounces off a large redwood in the middle of the grassy slope that's recently been mowed, mostly to keep people's feet from getting too wet from the tall grass in between the cabins by the river and the main house above, although it also helps with finding golf balls. "It's a great spot, a great way to get out of the rat race, I guess," he continues, adding that he also enjoys kayaking down the river and fishing in his free time, but there's never much of that to go around and even less once the summer growing season starts.

"It's beautiful up here," Zach says, taking another swing. "A beautiful prison."

That night, we dine on spaghetti with meat sauce and enjoy a couple of bottles of red wine. Unlike a lot of pot farms in the Emerald Triangle, this place isn't just comfortable, it's downright luxurious. There's a wide-screen television set in the living room surrounded by oversized leather couches and a large, glass-topped coffee table, upon which rests a wooden salad bowl full of weed. Over the course of the evening, several large joints are rolled and smoked. Comedy

Central's late-night lineup of *The Daily Show* and *The Colbert Report* provides the visual entertainment. Watching approvingly over the scene is a framed print of Shepard Fairey's *Hope* poster of Obama that hangs on the wall near a woodstove.

Dave the horticulturalist gets the master bedroom since he's arguably been working the hardest, while Lucky ends up crashing on the couch in the living room. The tree trimmers retire to the trailer near the ravine where several redwoods lay stricken, ready to be chopped to pieces. The rest of the crew retires to the wood cabin with the tree growing through it, which turns out to be the oldest structure on the property. I fall asleep with the sound of the river lulling me into unconsciousness, wave upon gentle wave rushing downhill to the sea, slapping the shore just yards away.

– – – – –

The chain saws shred the morning silence shortly after breakfast, followed by the sound of the generator powering the wood chipper parked near the cabin by the river. For the next several hours, everyone on the property, with the exception of Dave, grabs fallen tree branches and tosses them in the chipper, which creates mounds of mulch on the edge of the clearing. The work stops when the drizzling rain, which began midmorning, turns to a downpour. We break for a lunch of homemade vegetarian burritos. Everyone lends a hand, either chopping tomatoes, onions, jalapenos, and cilantro for a zesty pico de gallo or helping heat up the tortillas and beans. An hour later, as if on cue, the sun pokes through the clouds and once again burns off the mist.

Although it's messy, difficult work, everyone's stomach is stuffed, and nobody complains. Last year's crew was another matter entirely, Lucky recalls. "Some of those guys were just a bunch of fucking whiners," he says. "This place is five-star. I mean, look at the house—it's got showers, it's got cable, it's got wireless. What more do you need? A lot of people working up here are lucky to be living in tents all summer and shooting food out in the forest to survive. That crew didn't realize how lucky they had it. Now they're calling back, trying to get jobs for this summer and being told they aren't needed."

According to Lucky, it takes two to three experienced trimmers all day to trim just four pounds of marijuana. That's why, at harvest time, the Emerald Triangle is swollen with hippie kids from all over the country eager to cash in on the hourly wages, knowing full well they'll get to smoke marijuana the entire time and, if they work hard, end up with a nice bonus, like an ounce or so of weed. All the general stores and pharmacies in the area sell out of trimming scissors.

"Right around the beginning of October, you'll see everyone that's ever been a cosmetologist getting hired in the mountains," Lucky adds. "They go hire all the Asian haircutters and hair trimmers, anybody that's good with scissors is what you want because they are fast and good and worth their money." It's even better when the hired help are attractive young ladies from Southern California, such as the girls Amber brought up with the cameras that turned out not to be cameras. "It's always fun to bring some hot chicks to sit in the sun with no clothes on or no tops on," he says. "It's something really sexy and natural. Chicks love it. Some chicks want to have the weed all over them. It's easy to find them."

Lucky says one of his favorite summer pastimes is to patrol the beaches of Southern California to finds girls to trim at his farm. "You just go around Huntington Beach in July and go up to them and say, 'Do you support the medical-marijuana industry?'" he explains. "If not, no problem. If yes, next question: 'Do you have a job right now? No? Okay, would you like to trim some weed up in the mountains and stay in a cabin for a week or two and maybe make $500 or $1,000 and come back home with a quarter-pound of weed? Come chill in the mountains!'"

At the end of last year's harvest, Anton and Lucky realized their trimmers had left more than fifty pounds of decent pot lying on the cutting-room floor simply because they were too lazy to trim it. The buds didn't go to waste; now, they're being rolled into joints several times per day and are expected to last through the summer. "You have to have a small, tight, trustworthy team," Lucky says. "You don't want a mutiny on your hands, or people ripping you off, or maybe just taking off and telling the cops [about the location]. It takes a lot of fucking work to run a farm like this."

That said, Lucky adds, the people who work at this farm—whether they sleep in the trailer, the unheated cabin by the river, or the main house—are all quite fortunate compared to the ones who have to camp out in the woods for a month or more. "There's a ranch down the road a ways that's run by a total fucking Nazi," he tells me. "His guys don't eat good and he leaves them way out in tents ten miles into the woods with hardly any food and they're out there trying to hunt and shoot their own birds and it's a whole different environment. He'll come up every once in a while and drop off plenty of food and make sure things are running tight, but meanwhile, these kids are surviving off almost nothing, boiling their own water."

Just as important as worker morale, Lucky says, is making sure the plants remain healthy and produce the highest-yield crop possible. This is the job of Dave the horticulturalist, who speaks in a soft, mid-Atlantic accent and always seems to have a pair of fingernail-trimming scissors in his hand, whether to clip unproductive branches off the pot plants he's growing or to snip up a joint's worth of weed when his work is done.

Dave has his portable stereo turned up so the plants can hear the Steely Dan he's playing above the deafening roar outside. He explains that the five-to-six-foot plants that fill the three green-houses were all tiny plants just six inches tall only four months ago; these are the Sour Diesel clones, which Lucky instructed him to reproduce. To clone a marijuana plant, Dave explains, you clip a branch from the original that contains three or four nodes, dip the twig in a rooting-hormone solution, clip the leaves to prevent them from sucking up too much water in the crucial first few days, and finally scrape the bottom of the stem to create injuries, which helps the new plant develop roots.

While the clones in the greenhouse are now almost ready for flowering, the next crop of clones is spread out on the deck and in the basement of the house, in dozens of fifty-cube trays, each square containing a pinch of soil and a single clone. The soil, Dave says, is called Formula 707—after an Emerald Triangle area code—and in the greenhouse, each plant is in a camouflaged plastic sack made by a Sacramento-based company called, appropriately enough, Camo Pots, which also has a small shipping office in Costa Mesa. "These bags are specifically for this area, where people are growing outside, in the woods," he says. "You have the bag, you open it up, it's got perforations in it, it's camouflaged, and you're ready to rock and roll.

"This is as tall as the plants will get," Dave continues. "We're pruning for production, high yield, and for airflow to prevent mold and diseases, so these plants are shorter and wider, with more ter-minal ends that have energy flowing to them. Right now, we're doing preventative care, so I'm pruning out insignificant growth that won't make much of a bud and is taking energy away from the rest of the plant. The first line of defense is a healthy, happy plant." This particular pot farm, Dave says, is well situated, because it's close to the river. The only danger is that it floods every once in a while along the river valley. Just a few yards away from the green-house, next to one of the cabins on the property, are the remains of the foundation of a windmill that used to be part of the town that existed on this stretch of the river until it was flooded out forty years ago.

"We're lucky," he says. "We often get an afternoon breeze. It comes up the river valley, so that helps a lot in the summer, but it still gets really hot, which is why we need the fans. Being down in the river valley, it's considerably hotter than it is at a higher elevation." Dave points at the tree-covered ridgeline overlooking the farm half a mile away and several hundred yards above us. "The trees around the valley up there are snow-covered in winter," he explains. "The snow comes down here two or three times a year, but it doesn't stick, and while we get a nice breeze, it's not too windy."

In about a week, the plants will be ready for "light-dep," pot-growing parlance for light-deprivation therapy. Because twelve hours per day is the magic amount of time plants need to begin flowering, the strategy is to use as much natural light as possible to provide a half-day of light, and then, when twelve hours is up, to immediately cover the plants under a plastic tarp, thereby tricking them into behaving as if it's now almost autumn, and therefore time to reproduce, which, in the case of pot, means to blossom into sticky buds.

"If you do this right, you get your crop earlier than you would otherwise," Dave tells me. "With two people and a decent system of winches and pulleys, it's pretty easy to do. And then in three months, you have big, beautiful, sticky buds, and all you have to do is dry them, cure them, and trim them."

Dave has been at the farm since last fall, just after the outdoor harvest ended. He rarely leaves the property, although once, during the spring rainy season, he came close to driving up the mountain when the river began to flood.

"Life here is beautiful," he tells me. "If you have the right personality, it's a lovely place to be. You're out here in the woods, excluded. There are four people in this whole valley. It's six miles to the main road—three up and three down. I've spent days here without even thinking of leaving."

－ － － － －

The foreman of the chain saw crew, Red, a lanky giant from Santa Cruz with sinewy arms and a weather-beaten face, is covered in sweat and sawdust. He's standing on the deck of the main house, examining his day's work now that the sun is starting to set in the exact spot he'd predicted, newly devoid of redwoods and open to the light. Red and Lucky are guzzling Bud Lights. Red is Lucky's cousin; he jokes that he's not necessarily the best trimmer in the Yellow Pages, but with an underground operation like this, you can't just let your fingers do the walking and hire anyone in the book.

"I almost thought they were going to blindfold me and my guys when we came up here," he jokes. "Then we figured, once we finished the job, they wouldn't let us leave and just feed us to the pigs. In this business, it's all connections; it's all word of mouth and grassroots. It keeps the money among the bros, so everybody has a vested interest."

The tree-trimming operation is guaranteed to expand the farm's growing potential, and that's worth celebrating, but whether the plants can provide everyone with a living ultimately depends on Lucky's ability to sell the weed once it has been successfully harvested. Although the level of quality of the marijuana is affected by countless factors, it helps to ensure the clones belong to the correct strain to begin with.

"There is nothing worse than spending six months of your time, money, and effort on a crop, only to realize you're growing the wrong fucking strain," Lucky says. "I have 140 pounds sitting in New York right now that's turning to powder because it's not the right strain. I can't move it for any price. It's a quarter of a million dollars worth of shit sitting in Manhattan that nobody can touch, and that's just so fucked-up."

On the other hand, Lucky has recently signed a deal with a nutrient company for $50,000 worth of product. "So I have a warehouse in San Francisco full of nutrients right now," he says. "The deal is that they'll give me these nutrients as long as I document everything thoroughly. Every Friday, they need a certain amount of video clips, photos, and content. This is a major responsibility to commit to for the next six months, and I have to fulfill it or I will screw myself and everyone else in this operation, which I do not want to do because in growing weed, one of your biggest expenses are the nutrients."

Lucky takes a big sip of his beer. "If all I had to worry about was unloading this weed, life would be a party," he says. "I could go stack money if that's all I had to worry about, but I've got obligations. That's why tomorrow, when I leave here, I'll be meeting a guy in San Francisco who has forty pounds and I know another guy who wants twenty-five pounds he wants to distribute to his collectives, and I'm going to put them together and get a broker's fee."

There's a radio on in the background. The reception all the way out here in the woods is sketchy, but the music manages to make it through. It's a show called *Radio Without the Rules*, which runs on Humboldt's KHUM station—not to be confused with KMUD, which is famous for broadcasting the whereabouts of the local sheriff's deputies and DEA units when they roll out on their raids—and the song is an cheerful skiffle tune by the Two Man Gentleman Band. "I wonder who you dream about when you put that reefer in your mouth," the song goes. "In my dream, you dream. You dream of me."

Looking west at the setting sun, Red clutches a cigarette between the tobacco-stained knuckles of his left hand and waves at the open space where five or so redwoods used to stand along the gulley until a few hours ago, when he chopped them down.

"We did good," he tells Lucky, belching loudly. "Now you can see all the way to the ridgeline, and the good thing is, we put all the debris down there in the gulley so you don't have to haul that any-where—and it'll stop anybody from hiking up that fjord and finding this fucking place. Nobody can get through that mess."

Protecting the pot farm is all well and good, but Lucky isn't look-ing at downed trees so much as the wide-open sky.

"That's just beautiful," he says. "Look at all that light, bro."

The official start of outdoor pot-growing season may still be a week away, but in this corner of the Emerald Triangle, summer has just begun.

11 | Racer X Rides Again

It's just before 9:30 AM on January 18, 2012. So far this morning, Racer X has weighed out three pounds of OG Kush marijuana.

Right now, about four hours into his shift inside the Big Kahuna club's delivery center, he's separating trimmed weed into eighth-ounce-sized quantities that he then dumps into small white-capped plastic cylinders, each of which is labeled with a purple and yellow sticker bearing the name of the club. He puts two of the eighth-sized containers in paper bags, along with a lighter and lollipop.

These bags will provide customers with their buy-one-get-one-free specials once the dispensary's front door opens early that afternoon. Because the club has been making such progress in the past few years since it opened its storefront in Costa Mesa, it now offers free eighths for every walk-in purchase of an equal amount.

Previously, you had to have a special VIP pass to receive a so-called "manager's discount" in order to qualify for a buy-one-get-one deal—except of course at the end of the month, when to insure that they were not turning an actual profit, the collective would

181

advertise special deals. Racer X had been at the building since 5:30 that morning. He's just coming down off the high of his first hit of cannabis sativa for the day when his buddy walks in the door with some important news: the DEA is about to raid the building.

Racer X's friend had found out what was happening just minutes ago from one of the girls who worked for the collective, verifying patients, who in turn had been called by her friend, who happened to live around the corner from the dispensary and saw several police cars sitting out front. When the Big Kahuna didn't answer his cell phone, he'd immediately driven to the boss's house, where he learned from the Big Kahuna's wife, who was alone at home with the couple's two young children, that the DEA had pounded on their door at 5:30 that morning and hauled away her husband in handcuffs.

Figuring there was no sense in sticking around waiting for the DEA to arrive, Racer X and his friend begin putting whatever marijuana they see laying around in a metal safe. Without saying a word, they walk outside, using the button on their keychains to unlock the doors of their two cars when several vehicles belonging to the DEA, ATF, Costa Mesa Police Department—even an Orange County PD K-9 unit—roar around the corner into the parking lot.

Racer X takes two more steps towards his car. A black car screeches to a halt a few yards away and a man jumps out. He points a pistol in Racer X's face.

"Don't go anywhere, buddy," he says.

Racer X raises his hands in the air. "I'm not going anywhere," he instinctively answers. "You got me."

The federal government's crackdown on California's medical-marijuana industry has finally arrived on the doorsteps of the Big Kahuna's club.

— — — — —

Racer X's capture had been a long time in the making.

For the past few years, the feds had watched as hundreds of dispensaries opened around the state, flooding the low-income neighborhoods of San Francisco, Oakland, and Los Angeles with stores decorated with green pot-leaf symbols in the window and signs advertising medical referrals so that anyone with twenty bucks in his pocket could get a doctor's recommendation and start puffing that same day. No city had so offended the federal government as Oakland, home to Richard Lee's world-famous Oaksterdam University and the nation's largest dispensary, Harborside, run by Stephen DeAngelo, star of his own Discovery Channel reality show, *Weed Wars,* which portrayed DeAngelo as a crusading hero, but at the same time revealed to the masses just how profitable the medical-marijuana business was. It had gotten too big, and had to be stopped before the industry didn't just have its own reality show but its own cable television network.

By October 2011, on one of my trips to the Bay Area, when I sought to speak with them, neither man would agree to an on-the-record interview. Lee, however, did arrange for an assistant to give me a tour of the school, which has trained seventeen thousand students in growing pot since 2007, as well as the industrial neighborhood he helped revitalize downtown. Oaksterdam University was housed in a tall brick building with a colorful mural on the side. The top floor has executive offices and storage areas, while the two lower floors are made up of classrooms and a growing room full of clones students had nursed from clippings: L.A. Confidential—an indica weed with an eight-week flowering time; Purple Kush, a heavy indica; and Mango, an indica-sativa hybrid with a ten-week flowering time.

According to my guide, all of the plants were technically the property of the collective's patients, including the wheelchair-bound patient Hannah White, who physically cannot grow her own medicine. "That's her plant," the assistant told me. "So technically, the students are acting as caregivers. They are not taking the plant home or testing the product. They are doing a good deed and at the end she comes in and thanks them so much for growing her medicine." Photos of every graduating class were hanging in the hallway, a row of portraits four high and about thirty feet long. Some of the classes were taught at remote locations, such as Michigan, L.A., and Sebastapol, she explained.

In the lecture hall nearby, a map of the world is stuck with countless pushpins. "We asked students to put pins on where they're from," my guide said. "We've had people fly in from everywhere—Brazil, Japan, Ecuador, Iraq, Iran. These are people who actually walked through our doors here. It's so cool, because Oakland is having this revitalization effort and we have all these students coming here, spending weeks here, eating here, getting parking tickets here. It's a lot of revenue."

It probably didn't help my request to meet with Lee or DeAngelo that the IRS had just hit Harborside with a $2.5 billion tax bill, or that a February 1, 2011, letter from Melinda Haag, the US Attorney for the Northern District of California, to John Russo, Oakland's city attorney, had just been made public for the first time. "Congress has determined that marijuana is a controlled substance," Haag wrote, "and as such, growing, distributing, and possessing marijuana in any capacity, other than as part of a federally authorized research program, is a violation of federal law regardless of state laws permitting such activities."

While Haag echoed President Obama's claim that the feds weren't going to go after sick patients, its office wasn't going to tolerate cities that sought to cooperate with large-scale distributors. "The Department is concerned about the Oakland Ordinance's creation of a licensing scheme that permits large-scale industrial marijuana cultivation and manufacturing," Haag continued. "Accordingly, the

Department is carefully considering civil and criminal legal remedies regarding those who seek to set up industrial marijuana growing warehouses in Oakland." The letter threatened to prosecute to the fullest extent of the law anyone who "knowingly" facilitated that activity, including "property owners, landlords and financiers."

On October 4, 2011, just a few weeks before I visited Oaksterdam, that letter was leaked to the press and the feds confirmed their intention to take down California's medical marijuana industry with a new round of asset-forfeiture lawsuits and threatening letters to landlords. The first of these letters went to landlords in Haag's district: Northern California, home to the Emerald Triangle and the epicenter of the nation's underground weed economy. Twenty-four hours later, the feds followed up by filing forfeiture proceedings against property owners throughout the state. One of the landlords hit with such a lawsuit was Yousef Ibrahim, the owner of the Lake Forest strip mall where eight marijuana dispensaries were operating, including Mark Moen's shuttered 215 Agenda club. The feds seized over $180,000 from Ibrahim's bank account. The City of Lake Forest had spent the past year—and more than $500,000 in legal fees—trying to fight the likes of Christopher Glew in court and evict the clubs, citing the fact that a Montessori school is located in the strip mall next door and a new state law bans such clubs from operating within six hundred feet of a school.

Glew and other attorneys for the clubs had managed to keep them open by arguing that because the city never bothered banning marijuana dispensaries, it had no right to shut them down. But just a day after the feds sued Ibrahim, all the clubs shut their doors, and despite protests at city hall by activist groups such as the Orange County branch of NORML, they never reopened. For some reason, meanwhile, it took the DEA half a year to get around to raiding Oaksterdam. It didn't happen until April 2, 2012, but it succeeded in driving Richard Lee out of the business. "I've been doing this a long time," he told the *Los Angeles Times* four days later. "Over twenty years . . . I kind of feel like I've done my time. It's time for others to take over."

In Costa Mesa, home to the Big Kahuna's club, the feds had also been invited in by city hall, the agency's preferred method for raiding dispensaries. Just two years before the DEA raided the club, the city appeared to be on the verge of passing an ordinance that would effectively legalize marijuana dispensaries. One of the dispensary owners, Sue Lester, had even parlayed her cannabis activism into a campaign for city council on the issue, but had lost that campaign, which in retrospect was a high-water mark for the cause of cannabis in Costa Mesa. Since her defeat, the city's new political leaders, a raft of conservative Republicans, declared their intention to destroy the city's public-employee unions, privatize as many city services as possible, and lay off half the workforce. To say they backed away from the notion of regulating marijuana within city limits would be to grotesquely understate the facts. To begin with, they refused to meet with the Big Kahuna's lobbyist, Max Del Real, while at the same time the city's cops mounted their harassment of collectives.

Dispensaries began racking up fines of thousands of dollars per month. Code-enforcement officers accompanied by narcs would show up without notice, writing the clubs tickets for violating the city's business code and scaring customers. On May 6, 2011, Orange County Superior Court Judge David Chaffee ordered the closure of four Costa Mesa cannabis clubs, as well as several massage parlors, all of which were operating in the same building as Lester's dispensary, Herban Elements. The order also prevented any new cannabis clubs from operating at that address by specifically prohibiting "medical-marijuana sales, dispensing, cultivating, possession or distribution" at the address.

At a hearing a few weeks later, Glew managed to overturn the order by presenting evidence that the quartet of cannabis clubs were complying with state law, and therefore, the city has no right to shut them down. "There have been code violations that the city has cited, and we'll show the court that all of those issues have been rectified," Glew told me. "We have the right to operate these collectives under state law, and to ban them outright is a violation of their rights under the health and safety code." For her part, Lester complained that she wasn't given any time to respond to the city's declaration that her club was a nuisance. "It's not an issue of being fair, but doing what's legal," she said. "If you look at Costa Mesa's municipal code on declaring someone a nuisance, you have to issue a notice, give reasonable time to correct, the city council should hold a hearing, and then they can move through the court to abate the nuisance. I wasn't given reasonable time to respond. The whole thing stinks, and if they can do this to someone like me, they can do it to anybody, and that's not right."

Lester ended up closing her dispensary a few months later, having run out of hope that the city would act in good faith. She was right to be cynical. On October 26, 2011, City Attorney Tom Duarte sent a letter to the US Department of Justice begging for the feds to step in and arrest the pot purveyors. "We believe that by working together with the US Department of Justice we can eradicate these illegal businesses from our city," he wrote. "In our opinion, twenty-seven dispensaries in a 16.8-square-mile area constitute mass cultivation and distribution of marijuana."

Duarte wasn't acting alone—he had already cleared the confidential correspondence with the city council, including Mayor Gary Monahan, who nonetheless continued to provide lip service to the concept of rapprochement with the cannabis clubs. On January 15, Monahan, who owns the popular bar Skosh Monahan's in Costa Mesa, appeared on a local cannabis-themed radio show hosted by Robert Martinez, a former US army medic and owner of one of cannabis clubs, Newport Mesa Patients Association. "It's like the wild, wild West out there," he said on the show, whose other guests included prominent Orange County cannabis activists. "Everybody's doing whatever they want to do. You've got some really good dispensaries; you've got some really bad dispensaries that are just out for a quick buck. . . . There're a lot of good ones that we want to support."

Exactly three days later, the DEA descended on Costa Mesa.

During the radio show, Monahan had given no hint of what was about to happen. He later claimed he didn't know the exact timing of the coming raid, although he didn't indicate this on the pot-themed radio show because it went off the air after the station manager claimed he'd been threatened with criminal action by the FBI—something which, if true, would indicate that the feds were serious about their threat to go after media businesses, including magazines, newspapers, and radio and television stations that took money from advertisers engaged in illegal marijuana commerce.

The Justice Department also sent warning letters to the owners and operators of nearly three-dozen clubs in Costa Mesa and Newport Beach, giving them fifteen days to shut down (some already were shuttered), and filed asset-forfeiture proceedings against the owner of the building where Lester's shop had operated and where three clubs were still open. Just a week earlier, they'd filed a similar lawsuit against the building that houses the Alternative Medicinal Cannabis Collective (AMCC) in an unincorporated part of Covina, as well as issued more warnings to landlords and cannabis clubs elsewhere in Southern California where, the feds claimed, a total of seventeen stores were operating. Those letters warned that the stores were operating in violation of federal law and that they had just fifteen days to shut down.

Besides the Big Kahuna's club and the two local pot growers that were supporting it, where feds seized more than one thousand plants, the DEA hit a cannabis dispensary and grow facility in Costa

Mesa called Otherside Farms. Chadd McKeen, the farm's operator, had boasted to Costa Mesa Code Enforcement personnel that
he intended "to make so much money" at the location that he was
going to give the city of Costa Mesa a "donation" of up to $500,000
every year that would help the city stave off layoffs, according to the
Justice Department's press release on the raid.

The Big Kahuna was sound asleep when the DEA knocked down
his door. "They came in at 6:00 AM and pointed a machine gun at my
head," he told me. "They tossed up my shit and smashed my safe, they
took any and all paperwork." The agents seemed apologetic about
the interruption. "They kept saying the worst was over and that they
were sorry they had to do this in front of the neighbors," he said.

Along with $20,000 in cash that Racer X claims belonged to the
Big Kahuna's wife, whose father had just died, the feds seized the
keys to the club. "They took the keys to my club and the cannabis,"
he said. "The only two clubs they hit were paying taxes and providing payroll. All the illegal clubs not doing that got fifteen days to
move to Santa Ana. If I knew they were going to do it like that, I
would have done it illegally."

A couple of Costa Mesa cops who had accompanied the feds on
the raid of the Big Kahuna's house took him to the city jail, where
he spent the next several hours before being released without any
charges—although he did receive a warning that federal prosecutors could charge him any time in the next three years. They also
admonished him not to engage in selling any more marijuana.

Racer X and his friend, meanwhile, were sitting handcuffed inside
the delivery building, which the DEA mistakenly had believed was
a grow house. "Where are your plants?" they asked. Although he'd
spoken so far only to demand an attorney and indicate his refusal to
provide any information besides his name, Racer X finally answered.
"This is just a delivery area," he told them. "Nobody can come in
here except the drivers and the employees.

"You mean I can't come in here and buy marijuana?" one of the feds asked.

"No you can't," Racer X responded. "And if you look, there's no sign out front saying you can do that or saying anything about marijuana being in here."

The feds hauled two safes outside onto the sidewalk, despite assurances from Racer X and his friend that one of them was empty. Because they didn't have the keys to the safe, the feds called up the Costa Mesa Fire Department to saw them both open. Racer X recognized one of the firemen as a sergeant he'd met just a few weeks earlier, when he'd dropped off a few hundred toys that had been donated by members of the collective for the department's charity drive.

"He was a good dude," Racer X says. "He came up to me and was like, 'Dude, just give me the code to the thing and I'll open it,' but I told him there was nothing in there. Sure enough it took them ten minutes to open it and I heard someone yell, 'What's in there?' There was nothing."

Four hours later, the feds had seized several pounds of marijuana waiting to be delivered, as well as several thousand dollars, a mountain of paperwork, and other "evidence." They left without arresting either Racer X or his friend—but not before returning to them their own personal stashes of marijuana, which they were legally entitled to smoke, although under state, not federal, law.

The Big Kahuna club opened again for business the very next day, and stayed open for the next two weeks, until the club's landlord told the Big Kahuna that he'd received a threatening letter from the federal government and had no choice but to evict him. "They told him he couldn't rent property to any marijuana collectives for the next four years," the Big Kahuna says. "I wanted to fight it because I've got the best attorney in the county on retainer, but this must be his only income property, because he said no way, we had to go."

After two years of selling marijuana out the front door of its walk-in dispensary, the club had now gone full circle—straight back to delivery only. Overnight, the Big Kahuna had to lay off twenty-five employees who had been earning a salary of ten dollars per hour or more plus health benefits, leaving just a core crew of veteran workers including Racer X with jobs.

"For about two months after the raid it was awesome," the Big Kahuna told me. "Delivery was killer. But then everyone else started doing deliveries." After three months, the club's sales volume had been cut in half. "Now on Weedmaps there are twenty-five or thirty delivery companies in Costa Mesa, so there's a lot of competition, and not everyone wants deliveries anyways." The only people who benefited from the DEA raid, he reckons ruefully, are regular crooks. "The street life was dead, because we came along and sucked all the people off the street," he says. "All the guys out there slinging weed on the corner just got their jobs back—no payroll, no sales tax. Just the way the cops want it."

But the Big Kahuna has a plan to bounce back into legitimacy. He and those from what's left of the cannabis collectives in Costa Mesa have banded together to gather signatures to put a measure on some future city ballot that would legalize dispensaries again, effectively overturning the city's ban and offering some measure of protection against the local officials and federal drug agents intent on driving them out of business. He and several of his now-part-time or unemployed former workers, including Racer X, have been spending at least five days per week sitting at tables in front of Trader Joe's and other supermarkets, asking customers if they support medical marijuana and if so, would they please sign a petition to that effect. They've also been walking door to door, canvassing neighborhoods.

Although the Big Kahuna estimates that they're halfway to their goal of six thousand signatures—recently gathering three hundred in one weekend alone—it's still an uphill battle. It doesn't help, he adds, that everyone at the collective, including him, is looking for a day job. "The whole medical-marijuana thing feels like a lost cause," he concludes. "If the club was up and running, I'd have a bunch of weed warriors out there getting signatures. Instead, I'm sitting in front of grocery stores all day. I got a text from one of my guys today saying DUDE, I'M NOT FEELING THE CAUSE. Great. The ship is sinking, Rome is burning, and everyone's drinking and partying to the end while we go down in flames."

– – – – –

Six months after the raid, I'm sitting at a heavily scuffed, round wood table in the living room of a second-story apartment unit at a complex just a quarter-mile away from the Big Kahuna Club's former delivery headquarters. Racer X is seated in a chair across from me, leaning forward, intently focused on the plastic Zig Zag joint roller that he holds with both hands, expertly manipulating it in such a way that the large pile of shake leftover from the trimmed weed for that week's deliveries will soon transform itself into a week's worth of thank-you joints.

It's a highly labor-intensive customer-loyalty reward program, but nowadays pot clubs have to go that extra mile to stay in business, and besides, Racer X has nothing better to do. It's 1:30 PM and the club, which has now been downsized to this apartment unit, has been open for deliveries for half an hour. So far today, though, the club's one remaining telephone line (at its height six operators were standing by) remains stubbornly silent. His friend and coworker, who had been sleeping in the delivery building until the DEA raided it, now sleeps here, but at the moment he's watching an Angels game on the flat-screen television mounted on the wall. Finally, the phone rings, and Racer X heads out the door to deliver an eighth-of-an-ounce of weed to one of his new customers, a cheerful Italian-American furniture restorer.

Instead of the beat-up pickup truck he drove two years earlier, Racer X now drives a trendy sports car, and there's no oversized talking GPS system mounted on his dashboard, such a device having pretty much been obviated by his new talking iPhone 4. "When you first came with me, I was fumbling with that damn GPS system," Racer X recalls, chuckling. "Now I have not only mastered the GPS system, I don't even use it, because I know where the fuck I'm going. This is the ninth delivery since Monday where I haven't had to use my GPS system. It's all to the same group of people."

If Racer X gets five deliveries in a day, he considers himself lucky—even though, like all the members of the collective, he's not on salary anymore, and gets only a five dollar commission for each eighth he delivers. "The new patients we get are all older people, really friendly," Racer X says as we make the drive. "There aren't any scary people anymore. When I first started doing this, when you were there, I was freaking out and scared because I didn't know if someone was going to shoot me. We could show up somewhere and that could possibly happen."

Nowadays, with the DEA crackdown, Racer X continues, people will do anything to stay on his good side. "I've gone to places where someone wasn't around and I've waited and waited and go to the next delivery, and they call and I'm like, 'Dude, you are now at the end of the list. If they argue, guess what? You are now off the list. Don't call."

If anything, Racer X says, he often felt more worried while working the storefront dispensary. His most recent close call happened several days after the DEA raid, when a Latino waltzed in the front door with no doctor's recommendation but a freshly shaved scalp and a Lakers shirt that revealed a pair of bare arms covered in gang tattoos. "Hey man, I need weed," the guy had demanded. "Can't you hook me up?" Racer X feigned brotherly commiseration. "You know dude, I really can't," he apologized. "I just had the DEA climb up my ass a week ago." The conversation ended right there with those three letters. "I feel you," the gangster replied, rushing out the door.

Then there was the time before the raid when an Australian guy showed up for one of the Big Kahuna Club's buy-one-get-one-free parties, when the collective would hire a taco truck to park out front and pass out free food to members. Racer X was standing in the parking lot out front, greeting incoming customers. First the guy tried to walk straight into the dispensary, but when Racer X, realizing he was a newbie, told him he needed to fill out some membership forms and get verified before he could purchase any pot, the customer balked. "Instead, he starts asking me for blow, acid, and other stuff," Racer X recalls. "We told him to have a free taco and try the bars or the Grateful Dead shows." The Aussie was insistent enough that Racer X remembered the conversation when, two days later, an off-duty cop rolled up in front of the shop and started taking pictures of him.

Delivering weed still brings Racer X his fair share of strange customers, though. His favorite involves a large African American man who inherited an even larger sum of money from his recently deceased mother. "He was a really nice guy," Racer X recalls. "He was living at this really nice hotel in Newport Beach at the time, but was traveling all over Southern California, staying in nice hotels and trying to smoke as much weed as possible. We're in the lobby and the guy is busting open an eighth right there, and I'm like, 'Hey you really shouldn't do that here.' He's like, 'Why not? It's legal, right?' That was freaky. I really don't need people bringing police to me."

After dropping off the eighth for the Italian furniture restorer, Racer X and I grab lunch at a cheap taco joint. No more deliveries have been phoned in, so there's no place to go and no need to hurry back to home base. Racer X is about halfway through his fish taco when there's a lull in the conversation and he finally opens up about his raging midlife crisis. "When I started doing this, I was just trying to help [the Big Kahuna] out," he reflects. "Then it came to the point where I was starting to make some good money and things were growing so fast that I was making good money and getting health benefits. So I jumped from my job of fourteen years to do this. I climbed up the corporate ladder and the ladder got pulled from underneath me. I'll be lucky if I make forty dollars today."

Fortunately, Racer X left his grocery-store job on friendly terms, so if the deliveries dry up, he figures he can always go back there. But meanwhile, he's on unemployment, and he lives in his mom's house. Because she's retired, between the two of them they can barely cover the mortgage; bills pile up week after week and go unpaid. "The loan modification for my house got denied," he adds. "The form said, 'Are you secure in your job?' and 'How are your prospects for the next year?' I am not secure in my job and my prospects for the year are not good."

Although he really doesn't want to go back to stocking groceries, Racer X sees only one other option, assuming the federal government's marijuana crackdown continues: quit driving for the Big Kahuna Club and get into business with his own supplier. He's got a friend who lives in Humboldt County, deep inside the Emerald Triangle, and ever since the feds started busting dispensaries and raiding their grow houses in Southern California, the guy's been making twice-monthly trips down the 101 freeway. "He's a mule," Racer X explains. "The first three hours heading south are the scariest, but he doesn't have long hair anymore and he drives a nice car and plans it so that he doesn't hit too much traffic."

Until now, I'd always figured that Racer X was just another link in the vast and multi-layered distribution network of weed-runners who transport America's biggest illicit agricultural crop from the

Emerald Triangle to customers in Southern California and beyond. Now, suddenly, it's obvious that despite the DEA's raid just weeks ago, that same network is still as alive as ever, and the only question is whether it will involve him, much less the Big Kahuna or anyone else. One thing is for sure, though: weed running will never die. "I really don't think we've seen the last of it," Racer X says. "I don't think it's over yet."

As long as people smoke weed, which they always will do, Racer X figures that there will be a way to profit from it. "I can go into business for myself," he says, dreaming out loud. "Fuck forty dollars a day. I can pull some money out of my retirement fund, do advertising, get a website up. I could do this for the rest of my life."

When Racer X finishes his fish taco, we drive back to an apartment full of weed that's just waiting to be delivered.

Epilogue

When I set out writing this book, I never imagined that by the time I was finished, the federal government would have launched a massive crackdown on California's medical-marijuana industry. In dozens of interviews with sources at all levels of the industry, the idea that the momentum building in the past few years could so quickly crumble never came up. It was taken as an a priori assumption among the weed runners who I traveled with that the businesses they were creating and the markets they were opening were the economic equivalent of new "facts on the ground," to borrow the military-diplomatic term for something that could not so easily be reversed. Looking back, those who placed the most faith in the notion that what they were trying to accomplish wouldn't backfire on them in a big way tended to fare the worst.

Mark Moen, who could have spent decades behind bars after being arrested with a large quantity of marijuana and cash while running back and forth between the Emerald Triangle and his dispensary in Southern California, wisely took a plea deal. On March

5, 2012, he pled guilty to seventy-three counts of money laundering, four counts of selling marijuana, two counts of possessing it with the intent to sell, and one count of possessing more than $100,000 in cash from "narcotics proceeds." In addition to all that, Moen's plea deal required him to admit to a pair of sentencing enhancements: laundering more than $150,000 in cash and "crime-bail-crime," which is a fancy way of saying that Moen was on already on bail for a previous crime when he was arrested again. He received a much lighter sentence than if he'd risked a jury trial: just three years in state prison. And since he'd already spent most of that time behind bars awaiting trial, his sentence actually amounted to just two years of probation.

Steele Smith also wisely reached a plea deal in his medical-marijuana case that allowed him to avoid any further prison time whatsoever. Meanwhile, he developed a THC pill called Idrasil, which he hopes to market to elderly-care facilities and hospices as a palliative.

The Green Spot boys are still in business delivering weed in the Bay Area, although Christopher Glew, who continues to have no shortage of pot-related criminal defense cases, reports that Hoyt had an unspecified falling-out with El Machino, possibly the result of El Machino eating too many marijuana bars.

Long Beach eventually passed a ban on pot clubs, enforced with raids that seem to number one or two per week. Despite this, there are still numerous dispensaries operating in the city—they tend to shut down after being raided and then reopen—including several clubs that mysteriously have never been raided. Although sources close to the city confirm FBI agents have conducted interviews about allegations of corruption, no charges have been filed against any city official for taking bribes from marijuana clubs or their attorneys.

Joe Byron and Joe Grumbine are still awaiting their second trial at this writing, but Grumbine had the misfortune of being stopped by police while out on bail and possessing eight ounces of marijuana near his home in Riverside. That weight happens to be the largest legal amount you can possess under California law, and even though he wasn't arrested, he still violated the terms of his bail. Grumbine spent the Thanksgiving holiday behind bars after he showed up in a Long Beach courtroom for a November 13, 2012, trial-scheduling hearing. Assuming the Grumbine-Byron case does go back before a jury and they lose again, both men face several years behind bars for selling marijuana.

Lucky is, well, lucky. The last time I saw him he was filming a reality show at a phony dispensary in Anaheim, one that had just been set up for the cameras that very day. He's busy developing a new line of plant nutrients for the medical-marijuana industry, as well as a type of snack chip that he's hoping to market to the extreme sports crowd.

Racer X? Not so lucky. His friend the Big Kahuna still runs a delivery service, but on an ever smaller scale. He and Racer X no longer work with each other. Part of the problem is that Racer X can't drive—he had to sell his car to pay the bills. At this writing, the bank that holds the mortgage on the house he shares with his mother was threatening to foreclose. He's still debating whether to go back to stacking groceries or try to somehow eke out a living in the marijuana game.

Just when things looked as if they couldn't get much bleaker for marijuana, though, American democracy stepped in and saved the day. On November 6, 2012, Washington and Colorado became the first two states in American history to legalize marijuana for recreational purposes. Under the new laws, adult residents in both states can now possess up to an ounce of marijuana without any fear of arrest, and more importantly, the laws call for each state to develop rules and regulations that will outline how people can legally obtain their marijuana—something that California, with its maze of dispensaries and delivery services, never managed to accomplish.

In Washington, even before Initiative 502 became law on December 6, 2012, prosecutors immediately flushed hundreds of misdemeanor marijuana-possession cases out of the legal system by dropping all charges against the defendants. The Seattle Police Department, for its part, seemed to relish the fact that it finally had a clear direction on pot policy. Ever since a citywide ballot proposal in 2003 called on city cops to make enforcing the federal ban on pot smoking its lowest law-enforcement priority, officers had to use their own judgment on whether or not to make an arrest. Now, the law is much clearer, as the Seattle PD's in-house blogger Jonah Spagenthal-Lee noted in a post published immediately after the election results came in: "Marijwhatnow: A Guide to Legal Pot-Smoking in Seattle."

"The people have spoken," he wrote, before providing answers to several important questions about the new law, such as "What happens if I get pulled over and I'm sober, but an officer or his K-9 buddy smells the ounce of Super Skunk I've got in my trunk?" (Answer: "the smell of pot alone will not be reason to search a vehicle.") As if nodding to the surreal notion of the police providing tips on legal weed smoking, Spagenthal-Lee ended his Q&A session with a video clip from *The Hobbit*: Gandalf the wizard and Bilbo Baggins, the wandering hobbit, smoking their pipes.

In Colorado, prosecutors also immediately dismissed hundreds of misdemeanor pot possession cases involving people arrested with an ounce or less of marijuana or six or fewer plants. Governor John Hickenlooper, who clearly understands a thing or two about the munchies, quickly warned residents not to "break out the Cheetos or Goldfish too quickly," because there was no guarantee the feds were going to stop their pot crackdown just because of some silly vote. Less than a week after the election, Hickenlooper held an eleven-minute teleconference with US Attorney Eric Holder and other federal officials, the details of which neither side would divulge beyond the fact that all concerned considered the matter extremely important to resolve as quickly as possible. "Everyone shared a sense of urgency and agreed to continue talking about the issue," Hickenlooper's spokesman, Eric Brown, said in a November 10 press release.

As of this writing, only a few months after the election, it's still too soon to tell how the federal government plans to proceed. At the National Association of Attorneys General annual conference on February 26, 2013, US Attorney General Eric Holder announced that the Justice Department was close to reaching a decision. "We are, I think, in the last states of that review and are trying to make the determinations as to what the policy ramifications are going to be, what our international ramifications are," Holder said, adding that an announcement would be made "relatively soon." But even before the votes in Washington State and Colorado happened, sources of mine who'd tried and failed to prosper in California's medical-marijuana industry had already begun flocking to Colorado in search of gainful employment, including Amber, who survived Lucky's scheme to ship "cameras" north to the Emerald Triangle. She and others interviewed for this book are now in Colorado, helping to implement the new state law's apparent mandate to create a legal marketplace for recreational marijuana.

Another source of mine posted a desperate message on Facebook, warning her friends, including Amber, not to fall prey to the same naïve sense of entitlement that plagued those who fell victim to California's experiment with medical marijuana. "Winning a battle doesn't mean victory," she wrote. "Federal Law needs to change before we can truly see progress. Ask all California medical marijuana patients sitting in federal prison, on charges equal to heroin dealers, what California laws did for them!

"I don't mean to be a buzzkill for all those Californians migrating to Washington and Colorado," she continued. "But let me remind you that regardless of state laws, the feds will come kicking down your door, waving guns in your face. They will take your children, your assets and your freedom—over a plant."

Index

NICHOLAS SCHOU is the author of *Kill the Messenger: How the CIA's Crack Cocaine Controversy Destroyed Journalist Gary Webb* (Nation Books, 2006), which Focus Features is currently making into a movie starring Jeremy Renner, and the *L.A. Times* bestseller *Orange Sunshine: The Brotherhood of Eternal Love and its Quest to Spread Peace, Love and Acid to the World* (Thomas Dunne, 2010).

Schou is the managing editor of *OC Weekly*, an alternative newspaper in Orange County, California, and an investigative reporter who has covered the US war on drugs and the medical marijuana movement for the past seventeen years. He is the winner of numerous journalism awards including Best American Crime Reporting 2008, and his investigative reporting has led to the release from prison of wrongfully convicted individuals as well as the conviction and sentencing to prison of a Huntington Beach mayor.

Schou lives in Long Beach, California with his wife and son.

ALSO AVAILABLE FROM CHICAGO REVIEW PRESS

The Politics of Heroin:
CIA Complicity in the Global Drug Trade

Alfred W. McCoy

34 B/W Photos · 5 Charts · 13 Maps

"A fascinating, often meticulous unraveling of the byzantine complexities of the Southeast Asia drug trade . . . a pioneering book."
—*The New York Times Book Review*

Trade Paper, 734 Pages · ISBN-13: 978-1-55652-483-7 · $32.95 (CAN $49.95)

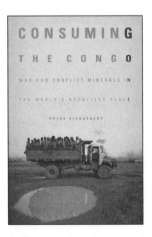

Consuming the Congo:
War and Conflict Minerals in the
World's Deadliest Place

Peter Eichstaedt

45 B/W Photos

"Eichstaedt provides counterpoint and a glimmer of hope in the form of possible reforms and legislations that could restore order to a devastated region."— *Publishers Weekly*

Cloth, 272 Pages · ISBN-13: 978-1-56976-310-0 · $24.95 (CAN $27.95)

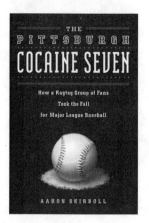

The Pittsburgh Cocaine Seven:
How a Ragtag Group of Fans Took the Fall for
Major League Baseball

Aaron Skirboll

12 B/W Photos

"A must-read for any sports fan willing to peel back the phony veneer often portrayed by the leagues and read a true behind-the-scenes story of corruption within professional sports, *The Pittsburgh Cocaine Seven* should be next on your reading list."— *San Francisco Examiner*

Cloth, 288 Pages · ISBN-13: 978-1-56976-288-2 · $22.95 (CAN $25.95)

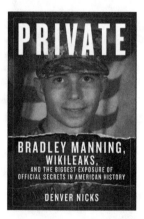

Private:
Bradley Manning, WikiLeaks, and the Biggest
Exposure of Official Secrets in American History

Denver Nicks

15 B/W Photos

"In telling the story of how the intelligence analyst Bradley Manning came into contact with the self-promoting anti-secrecy radical Julian Assange under the pressure cooker of the Iraq war, Denver Nicks has written a page-turner that reads like a cyberthriller. It's simultaneously a coming-of-age story, a coming-out story, an X-ray of American culture in the Homeland Security era, a well-researched history of espionage, an exposé of the routinized cruelties of the 21st-century US military, and a meditation on the human costs of the cult of secrecy."
—Ned Sublette, author of *The World that Made New Orleans*

Cloth, 288 Pages · ISBN-13: 978-1-61374-068-2 · $24.95 (CAN $27.95)

Available at your favorite bookstore,
(800) 888-4741, or www.chicagoreviewpress.com

CHICAGO REVIEW PRESS